Total Wealth

Lifetime Wealth and Lifelong Security

Mac Barnes

**CAPITAL
PRESS**

Washington, D.C.

Library of Congress Cataloging-in-Publication Data

Barnes, Mac.
   Total wealth : lifetime wealth and lifelong security / by Mac Barnes
    p. cm.
   Includes index.
   ISBN 0-89526-235-5
   1. Investments. 2. Securities. 3. Stocks. 4. Financial security.

  HG4521 .B39 2000
  332.63'22—dc21

00-067350

Published in the United States by
Capital Press
A Regnery Publishing Company
One Massachusetts Avenue, NW
Washington, DC 20001

Visit us at www.regnery.com

Distributed to the trade by
National Book Network
4720-A Boston Way
Lanham, MD 20706

Printed on acid-free paper
Manufactured in the United States of America

10 9 8 7 6 5 4 3 2 1

Books are available in quantity for promotional or premium use. Write to Director of Special Sales, Regnery Publishing, Inc., One Massachusetts Avenue, NW, Washington, DC 20001, for information on discounts and terms or call (202) 216-0600.

To my Dad

Contents

FOREWORD

DURING MY YEARS ON WALL STREET, I learned a fundamental truth of investing: keep it simple. Time and time again, I've seen complex and supposedly sophisticated theories of investment proved worthless by their performance record—the only thing that really matters. Smart investing boils down to three things:

    (1) predictions of market performance must be
        based on history
    (2) set realistic investment goals
    (3) prepare to endure short-term volatility

Mac Barnes has taken these principles and applied them just as you would expect from a trained efficiency expert. He has provided a concise blueprint of how to safely get the most bang for your buck based on solid economic history and economic principles. Moreover, he provides professional details about investing and personal wealth management that make this book useful for both the beginner *and* experienced investor.

Take my advice: read this book. It's not only about creating wealth, it's about how to live a lifestyle that's economically sound and personally rewarding.

—Michael Bloomberg
CEO and Founder,
Bloomberg L.P.

INTRODUCTION

GUESS WHAT? Life is about living, not making money. Wouldn't it be nice not to worry about money? Then you could spend more time on the important things.

But you are not going to let go of the money thing unless you know that your money is well taken care of. We need to know that we are making the greatest use of every opportunity for profit that is available to us.

Think of what you could do today if you knew that your money was being managed optimally, earning the highest possible rates of return, and clearly outperforming other investment opportunities? And what could you do today if you could predict how much money you would have in the future, and if it was a large number?

People used to ask me, "How should I manage my money?" At first I gave seminars on "The Power to Get Wealth." Then I wrote a short article and now this book. While writing, doing the research, and managing my own money, a wonderful money management strategy serendipitously became apparent. Yes, you can accumulate large sums of money in your lifetime; it is not hard and anyone can do it.

What you are about to learn you can prove for yourself. All the evidence is within these covers. The goal is to educate and empower

INTRODUCTION

you to "go and do likewise." We do not assume that you have any experience in investing. Yet even the sophisticated investor will find a strategy that will become the benchmark against which all other investments are compared.

Finally, I am not a disciplined person. Therefore, anything that I ought to do, or should do, never works for me, because I don't do it consistently. The providential part of this strategy is you do not have to do anything. That's right; once you understand these concepts, you do very little.

Life is not about money; it's about you. We want investments that empower our lifestyle. We will address what most books on investment leave out—you. Most articles or books on money omit the rest of your world, the world outside the markets. People are born, get married, have children, grow old, retire, and then leave their wealth to their heirs. Is there an investment strategy that covers your changing life? And what is really changing? You still want to make money, no matter how old you are! If anything changes, it is that when you were younger you didn't need as much money as you do now.

If I am talking about you, raise your hand. You're going to enjoy this book. What is better than enjoying this book? Profiting from this book. We will do our best to achieve both goals.

PART 1:
THE BIG IDEA

CHAPTER 1

Accumulating a Million Dollars

WANT TO ACCUMULATE A MILLION DOLLARS IN YOUR LIFETIME? Would you like to give each of your children one million dollars? What you are about to read will change the way you accumulate wealth. With this information you can begin to accumulate wealth optimally. This will become the benchmark by which you judge all future investments. This chapter will give you a quick overview.

Pillar 1: Compound Returns

The first pillar of personal wealth is compounded returns on your investment. $10,000 invested at 14⅞% for thirty-five years becomes $1,280,000. Now, 14⅞% is interesting for two reasons. First your money doubles every five years if it is invested at 14⅞%. That means in five years $10,000 becomes $20,000, and after five more years (total: ten years) it becomes $40,000, and so on ($80,000, $160,000, $320,000, $640,000) until it reaches $1,280,000 after thirty-five years. And all that without adding a single penny to your original $10,000.

The second interesting thing about 14⅞% is that it is close to the return on common stocks for the past twenty years. We are using the S&P 500 Stock Index as a proxy for the stock market.

As of 10/31/00, the exact returns have been:

S&P 500 stock index return over the past 3 years	17.58%
S&P 500 stock index return over the past 5 years	21.64%
S&P 500 stock index return over the past 10 years	19.40%
S&P 500 stock index return over the past 15 years	17.47%
S&P 500 stock index return over the past 20 years	16.51%

Therefore, you can see that 14⅞% was a rate of return that you could have earned if your $10,000 had been invested in the S&P 500 Index.

Pillar 2: Asset Allocation

Can you keep all that money compounding for thirty-five years? Yes, you can, but most of us do not. Why? Because as soon as the refrigerator breaks we raid the savings account, and out goes our compound returns. The solution to this problem is to have two accounts. Let's call one your savings account, and you use it like most of us use our savings account: to save for a house or a car or to pay an unexpected bill. We will always need those savings dollars.

The second account we will call our Personal Endowment Account (PEA), and we never withdraw from that account. The money we put into the Personal Endowment Account we will never expect to spend. Of course, if we need it when we retire, we can use it, or if we experience a major disaster, we may resort to it. But if we are healthy and prosperous for the rest of our life, then we will leave it to our heirs. That's right; following this plan you will save a million dollars and never spend it in your lifetime, but you will be personally wealthy. Did anyone ever tell you, "You can't have your cake and eat it too"? Therefore, any money we put into the Personal

Endowment Account will remain there for our entire life, earning compound returns. This is pillar number two.

Fear not: Having a million without spending it does not mean that you can't enjoy life. How would you like to be well endowed? The lifestyle of a dowager could be yours. That simply means that your wealth grows faster than your expenses. We usually think of a dowager as an old rich widow living off her late husband's estate. But let's think of young, happy people living off their own personal endowments.

Pillar 3: Index Funds

In 1973 a Princeton University economics professor, Burton G. Malkiel, wrote *A Random Walk Down Wall Street*,[1] in which he proposed that the market averages would over time outperform active market participants. This is because Malkiel believes that markets are basically efficient. If markets are efficient, then people who try to beat the market will lose for two reasons: first, because trading generates high transaction costs, while following the market averages entails minimum transaction costs; second, and more important, active investors are frequently wrong, and their losses reduce their returns to below the average. It is very difficult to beat an efficient market.

In the same year one of the fathers of value investing, Benjamin Graham, said the same thing in his classic book, *The Intelligent Investor*. "Since anyone—by just buying and holding a representative list—can equal the performance of the market averages, it would seem a comparatively simple matter to 'beat the averages'; but as a matter of fact the proportion of smart people who try this and fail is surprisingly large. Even the majority of investment funds, with all their experienced personnel, have not performed so well over the years as has the general market."[2]

Perhaps as a result of these ideas, the Vanguard Index Trust 500 Portfolio was started in July 1976. This no-load mutual fund matches the S&P 500 Index. Over the past fifteen years, this fund has out-performed 86% of all equity mutual funds. Their annual fees are very low (0.18%) compared to most funds (average fees, 1.66%) because they make no investment decisions; they just mimic the S&P 500 Index. This index fund has a very low turnover; therefore, investors do not receive large taxable capital gains distributions.

Vanguard Index Trust 500 Portfolio (VFINX)		
Total Return and Performance Ranking versus All Other Equity Mutual Funds		
	Total Return	Percentile Ranking among All Equity Funds
3-year return	17.63%	top 28%
5-year return	21.64%	top 18%
10-year return	19.32%	top 25%
15-year return	17.28%	top 14%
Source: Morningstar, 10/31/00		

These results, while impressive, do not include taxes. When we look at after-tax returns, the index fund outperforms even more mutual funds.

Recently, Professor Malkiel told the Bloomberg Forum, "You *will* make money forgetting all the advice of Wall Street analysts and investing instead in equity index funds. Not *can* but *will*." Now, this professor has a track record to substantiate his theory. "What's amazing to me is how well it works," Malkiel says. The basic tenet remains the same as in 1973: public markets are innately efficient, so there's little point in trying to outguess them.

Now, consider the implications of this. Could we find a mutual fund that did better than the S&P 500 Index over the past fifteen years? Yes, but only 14% of equity mutual funds outperformed the

S&P 500 Index; 86% underperformed the index. And we have the advantage of looking back in time. But, Burton Malkiel and Benjamin Graham said that the S&P 500 would outperform most mutual funds before it happened. Now, can we pick the mutual funds that will outperform the market for the next fifteen years? That is more difficult. But if we believe that the stock market is innately efficient, then, if we pick the market average, we can expect to beat over 80% of the mutual funds in the next fifteen years. And we can make that prediction in advance and expect never to have to change our mind. Therefore, using index funds is our third pillar.

What does the S&P 500 Index consist of? It is the 500 leading companies in the United States. Therefore, we have invested in a diversified portfolio of the most successful companies. And since at any time in the future it will still be the 500 leading companies, we will never have a reason to change our mind.

Pillar 4: Deferring Taxes

Consider the tax cost to us of changing our mind. Let us suppose that we select a terrific mutual fund which performs well for fifteen years, and our $10,000 investment has become $80,000. But now our mutual fund is underperforming, and we decide to switch to another fund. When we sell the fund, our cost basis is $10,000, and we owe tax on a $70,000 capital gain. If capital gains are taxed at 20%, that is a $14,000 tax, leaving us only $56,000 to reinvest in the new mutual fund. You can see that we will *never* get to a million if we have to pay taxes every time we switch investments. But if we buy an S&P 500 Index fund, we will never need to switch; it is an investment that we can live with, and it will accumulate tax deferred because we never sell it. When we arrive at one million, our original investment is still $10,000. Therefore, by never switching funds we accumulate compound returns without paying capital gains taxes.

We exaggerated when we said you would "never" accumulate a million if you had to pay capital gains taxes when you switch investments. But how much will those taxes cost you? It depends on how many times you switch. But let's say you are following a similar plan, and every ten years you decide to switch mutual funds and therefore realize your accumulated gains and have to pay capital gains taxes. After thirty-five years you would have accumulated $631,090 instead of the $1,280,000 you would have accumulated if you had not switched funds every ten years. Most people, moreover, trade their investments more often than once every ten years. When you switch investments, you pay the tax, and this reduces total return (unless you are using an IRA or Keogh account). The deferral of capital gains taxes is our fourth pillar.

Also, suppose you switch investments because the fund or stock that you own is not beating the market. Since you are going to pay a significant capital gains tax if you sell a fund that has accumulated in value, most people wait to see if their fund will revive. This means that if your fund is underperforming, you will wait to see if it will start going up again. Finally, you bite the bullet and sell it. But in the meantime you have allowed an underperforming fund or stock to stay in your portfolio longer than you would have liked. Therefore, the most dangerous part of investing is switching investments: first, because it causes a tax bite; second, because we tend to hold on to losing investments; third, because we can't predict the future and don't really know what to buy next. Not to mention a fourth problem, which is that we must pay attention to the market and the condition of our portfolio at all times. Investing in index funds eliminates all four of these problems.

Combining Pillars 1 to 4

Can one earn superior returns by investing in the market average? Common intuition suggests that the market average beats only half of the market participants. But we have suggested that the market average will beat more than half. In addition, expenses and annual taxes are lower on the average index fund. Also, we can defer long-term capital gains taxes by limiting our trading. What is the combined result of all these advantages? This chart compares the after-tax and after-expense returns from investing for ten years in 363 equity mutual funds to similar returns from investing in an S&P 500 Index mutual fund. The vertical line in the center is the return on the S&P 500 Index funds; the distribution of equity mutual fund returns above and below the index fund returns comprise the black bars. For example, the bar immediately to the left of the heavy vertical line, "–2%" with the number "19" above it, indicates that nineteen equity mutual funds earned between 0% and 2% below the index fund return. We see that after expenses, annual taxes, and long-term gains, the S&P 500 Index funds beat all but twenty-six equity mutual funds (93%).

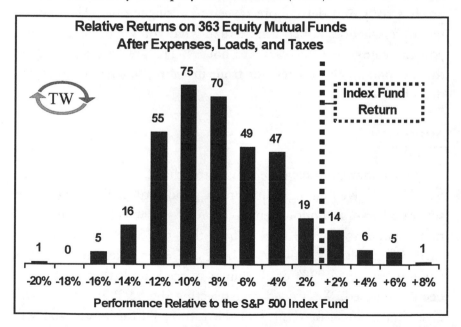

**Relative Returns on 363 Equity Mutual Funds
After Expenses, Loads, and Taxes**

Index Fund Return

Performance Relative to the S&P 500 Index Fund

Having identified a successful investment strategy, can we increase the amount of money that we put into this investment strategy?

Pillar 5: The Endowment Lifestyle

The endowment lifestyle is different from the save and spend lifestyle that most of us practice. We save for a car; then we spend our money. We save for a house; then we spend our money. We save to send our children to college; then we spend that money. Finally, we save to retire. Each time we spend what we save. But the endowment lifestyle keeps our savings invested. How would you like to have the compounded value of your car, your house, and your children's college tuition in your Personal Endowment Account (PEA)? How can we compare beating the market to beating the market with an account balance that is three or five or seven times larger than we would ever accumulate with a save and spend lifestyle? In addition, the endowment lifestyle improves our investment results by increasing our investment horizon. Long-term investments in index funds are less risky and defer more taxes for a longer time. The endowment lifestyle does not cost more than what you are doing now, and you can enjoy the same cars and houses. The greatest contribution to our total wealth comes not from investing but from modifying our lifestyle.

Summary

In summary, we have demonstrated that $10,000 will become $1,000,000 given enough time and a good return. We suggested a separate Personal Endowment Account, from which we will never make withdrawals. We have shown that the S&P 500 Index has earned high returns, close to 14⅞%, and after taxes and expenses has outperformed 93% of all similar mutual funds that could have been purchased. We argued that selecting the S&P 500 Index will give similar superior returns in the future. Furthermore, you will have no desire to switch out of the S&P 500 Index, which is in keeping with the long-term nature of this plan. Our strategy is to buy the index and hold it. Therefore, never selling your invested funds will defer your capital gains taxes, allowing your compound returns to accumulate. It also relieves you of having to become a market expert or having to follow the market at all times. In addition to this investment plan, the endowment lifestyle allows more dollars to remain invested. The combination of higher returns on a larger account balance for a longer investment period is phenomenal.

One key to this plan is starting. If $5,000 doubles to $10,000 in five years, then $500,000 doubles to $1,000,000 in the same five years. But getting to that first half million takes some time. You don't have to put aside $10,000 and wait thirty-five years to have one million. You could invest $5,000 and deposit $300 a month ($10/day) for twenty-five years. Or you could invest $10,000 and add $1,000 a month and have a million in eighteen years. Many people have the income, but it all gets spent on things that earn no return. We will demonstrate that the same people, with the same jobs, can enjoy the same luxuries, yet grow in total wealth.

The world in which we live has changed in the past century. People live longer than ever before. Individuals may live in retirement for thirty or forty years. We expect that we will live longer than the previous generation. What if we can continue to earn compound returns past retirement age until the end of our life? When we combine an endowment lifestyle with an extended lifespan and compound returns the results are staggering.

How about children or grandchildren? If this plan is started when a child is born, by the year he or she is thirty-five, he will have $1,200,000, and five years later it will be $2,400,000. At that time in his life he will not want to sell it because it will be all capital gains. Instead, he can borrow against it or just withdraw a small amount each year while the rest grows. Wouldn't we like it if our grandparents had done this for us?

What if the market goes down? This is a real life book, and we examine all the possibilities in detail. The stock market has gone down and will go down again. We will show how you can profit through the up markets *and* the down markets.

You will learn how far the market has dropped from its highs in every decline since 1914, and how long it took to go back up. We explain market-entrance strategies to minimize the possibility of buying at a market top. You will learn how to decide how much of your money to put into the market. We will demonstrate risk so that you will see and avoid risky situations.

We will also cover market-exit strategies to provide income for retirement while maximizing your total return. We will cover sheltering your future income from inflation. And we will demonstrate transactions that minimize future taxes on your PEA.

Total wealth includes not only making money but spending money and living a secure, worry-free life. We identify lifestyle risks that could threaten your investment success. We suggest lifestyle choices that reduce uncertainty. We present principles that will increase your lifestyle total return.

These principles of investing are not new. But combining classic investment principles with the index mutual fund brings benefits to the ordinary person that were not available in the past. You will learn how to earn high returns with low risk. To reduce the risks even more, we investigate each area where you could make a mistake. This book is not only about money; it is about educating you to manage your money correctly. We aim to give you the best education, and we will prepare you to succeed.

CHAPTER 2

Important Details

THESE DETAILS WILL HELP YOU UNDERSTAND INVESTMENTS. We love to skip the details because it won't change the main idea. But plowing through the details will give you a complete understanding of the subject, if only so you can display your expertise at social gatherings.

Not for Short-term Investments

An important detail is that as good as this plan sounds, it is not for short-term investments. The stock market could be down 25% or more in a single year. If you need this money back in one or two years you could have a significant loss. Over time the stock market has consistently moved up, but with a lot of fluctuations. If you are invested for a long time, the gradual uptrend will overcome the short-term fluctuations, and you will make money over the long term. Therefore, this is only appropriate for investment horizons over ten years. If you know that you will need this money soon, do not put it into the stock market. Should we say this twice? If you know that you will need this money sometime in the next five years, do not put it into the stock market!

13

Uninterrupted

Let us emphasize that this plan is based on compound returns. The money must continue to compound without interruption and preferably without paying capital gains taxes. Withdrawing money and then putting it back later will not achieve the same goals. For example, if your money doubles every five years, then in thirty years your money would double six times: 1 doubles to 2, 2 to 4, 8, 16, 32, and then 64 ($2^6 = 64$). (See Doubling Table.) If you take one dollar out of the Personal Endowment Account now, you are removing $64 in account value thirty years from now. Or if you take out $5,000 today, five years from now you need to put $10,000 back to stay even. But if you can imagine putting $10,000 back in five years, why not leave the account undisturbed and still put in money in the future? Also, when you make the withdrawal, you will owe taxes on your gains. That means that if you take out $5,000 today, five years from now you need to put back two times $5,000 plus two times the capital gains tax that you had to pay. To restate the point, allocate some money to a conventional savings account and allocate a reasonable amount to your Personal Endowment Account, and then leave the PEA undisturbed for the rest of your life.

Doubling Table
$2 = 2^1$
$4 = 2^2$
$8 = 2^3$
$16 = 2^4$
$32 = 2^5$
$32 = 2^5$
$64 = 2^6$
$128 = 2^7$
$256 = 2^8$
$512 = 2^9$
$1,024 = 2^{10}$
$2,048 = 2^{11}$
$4,096 = 2^{12}$
$8,192 = 2^{13}$
$16,384 = 2^{14}$
$32,768 = 2^{15}$
$65,536 = 2^{16}$
$131,072 = 2^{17}$
$262,144 = 2^{18}$
$524,288 = 2^{19}$
$1,048,576 = 2^{20}$

Income Dividends

When we spoke about accumulating returns tax free, we did not count the dividends earned on the S&P 500 Index. You would owe taxes on the dividend on the S&P 500 Fund, which is currently about

1.5% per year. In the early years this would be a small tax (unless you are using your IRA or Keogh account where the dividend income would be tax deferred). In Chapter 16, "Tax Strategies," we identify methods to defer or avoid several types of taxes.

IRA or Keogh Accounts

Another detail is that IRA or 401(k) accounts are retirement accounts, which means your gains and income will be tax deferred until you retire, and contributions are pretax. If you pay 40% in federal and state taxes and deposit $2,000 into your IRA, $800 is money that you would have had to pay in taxes. Therefore, you contribute $1,200 and the Internal Revenue Service contributes $800. This is a great benefit, and you should be using these accounts to make pretax savings and to defer all taxes on your long-term investments. Think of them as your Personal Endowment Account. But some people may wish to save more than the maximum allowed in an IRA or Keogh, in which case they need a taxable Personal Endowment Account.

Capital Gains Dividends

Mutual funds distribute capital gains from the trading that the fund does. Index funds are more tax efficient than actively managed funds.

The typical U.S. stock-fund manager generates 88% turnover in a given year, meaning that a stock is held on average for just over a year before it's sold. This brisk trading does little to promote tax efficiency since securities held for less than 12 months do not qualify for the lowest capital gains tax rate of 20%. If selling registers a short-term gain, the tax can add up. An investor in, say, a 31% federal bracket, after adding local taxes, forfeits nearly 40% of profits earned to Uncle Sam. Plus a manager must find another holding to replace the discard.[1]

As the investor, you will pay taxes on the short-term and long-term capital gains that mutual funds distribute to their shareholders. But index funds typically distribute much smaller gains because index funds have low turnover. The Vanguard Index 500 Fund had a turnover of 6%.[2] One of the top-performing funds for the past ten years, Fidelity Contra Fund, had a turnover of 165%,[3] meaning 165% of its holdings were traded in one year. It paid out taxable capital gains distributions of $10.22 per share in 1999; the average share price was $60.95. Would you rather have the price rise $10 on your mutual fund or receive a $10 taxable dividend?

Why do index funds have low turnover? Index funds mimic the index and do minimal trading. They are called passive investment managers. Because the market strategy of index funds is simple, you would expect their management fees to be lower also. On the other hand, active fund managers typically try to produce high returns. They are compensated based on how they perform. That explains why many actively managed funds have high turnover and are not tax efficient.

Outperform Every Year?

Another detail is that the S&P 500 Index did not outperform 84% of the equity mutual funds every year. To be exact, in the past fifteen years the index outperformed more than 70% of equity funds only seven times (or years): three years it ranked between 50% and 70% of all equity mutual funds; five years it ranked between 35% and 50% of all equity funds.[4] But over time the index outperformed 84% of all equity funds. Therefore, there will be years when owning the index does not look like a good strategy, but remember, in the long run the market averages do better than average. This is a key concept. If you drop out of this plan, you will never achieve those compound returns. Therefore, before you begin, expect fluctuations and expect to stick with the index for life. Dropping out when the market goes down or underperforms will surely give you below average returns.

Monitoring the Market

Another detail is that many people do not consistently monitor their investments. They put the money away and fail to look every day, or every week, or even every year to see how their investments are doing. If the money is invested for a child, it could be twenty years. If this describes you, then investing in the market averages solves the problem. The goal here is to pick an index fund and stick with it for life. There is no requirement that you actively monitor, or trade, your investments. In fact, this is one of its major luxuries. You put money into your Personal Endowment Account and let it grow without any having to worry or work trying to follow it.

CHAPTER 3

Taxes a Sure Thing!

SOMEONE SAID, "THE ONLY THINGS THAT ARE CERTAIN IN LIFE ARE DEATH AND TAXES." Do you think we can find a way to *profit* from taxes? What are the costs of our investment program? The costs are income taxes on dividends, taxable capital gains distributions, long-term capital gains taxes on successful trading, and mutual fund fees. How can we profit from taxes and fees? By long-term investing in index funds we minimize taxes and fees. Every fee that we don't pay and every tax that we don't pay increases our return relative to the way we used it to invest. In short, we can increase our return at the government's expense. Can we increase our return so much that we beat the active managers?

Mutual Fund Fees

First, let's look at costs. Not all mutual funds cost the same. And not all index funds cost the same. Is cost a relevant factor? Certainly cost is relevant in the extreme cases; no one wants to pay the highest cost. Unlike a stock, you pay a management fee to the manager of the mutual fund. In this respect, mutual funds are at a disadvantage compared to stocks.

When buying an index mutual fund, cost is independent of your real goal. If you buy shoes, you could justify paying more for better shoes. But there is no such thing as a better index fund. All index funds track the index. Therefore, higher costs reduce your return but bring you no benefit! Even with actively managed mutual funds, research has demonstrated no correlation between higher fees and higher returns. Therefore, even active fund investors cannot justify paying high fees.

Are there any standard charges? Long ago the standard charge for money management was 0.5% (½ of 1%) per year. That means that if you invest $1,000, you will pay $5 per year for management. If your $1,000 earns 10% which is $100, then the manager takes $5 and you keep $95. If your assets decline in a down market, the manager still collects the management fee.

Now, equity mutual funds have moved quite far from the traditional 0.5% fee. Some are less and many are more. These two graphs show actual mutual fund fees. The top graph (Equity Mutual Funds) shows that the majority of equity mutual funds charge more than 0.5%. The bottom graph (S&P 500 Index funds) shows that the majority of index funds charge less than 0.5%. For example, in the top graph on the next page, the bar on the right, "3.5% to 4%" with the number "15" above it, indicates that 15 mutual funds charge between 3.5% and 4% of total assets invested per year.

To create these charts we added the expense ratio and one-fifth of any sales load. (This averages the up-front sales charge over an assumed five-year holding period.)

The average annual expense over 749 equity mutual funds was 1.72%. The average annual expense over 28 index funds was 0.60%. Therefore, the average index fund costs 1% less than the average actively managed equity mutual fund. And eight of the index funds had annual expenses of less than 0.25%.

There are many types of fees. Some funds have a sales charge, also known as a front-end load, which is a one time charge deducted

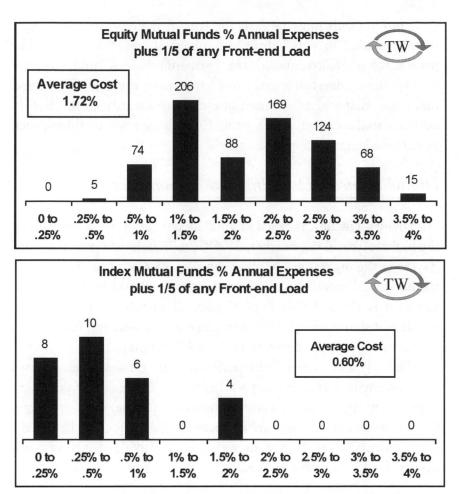

before your money is invested. The load, often from 3% to 6%, compensates the salesperson that sells you the fund. Funds that have no sales charge are called no-load mutual funds.

All funds have a management fee, also called the investment advisory fee, often ranging from 0.5% to 1.0%. In addition, some funds charge administrative and operating expense fees. Some funds have a distribution fee (a "12b–1" fee), which covers marketing the fund to new investors. Normally, the sum of the annual fees is published as the expense ratio. The expense ratio does not include any front-end load.

Mutual funds must publish the fees in their prospectus, which will be mailed to you before you invest if you ask for it. (The prospectus is always mailed after you purchase a fund.) Typical mutual fund advertising does not emphasize the fees. Therefore, make sure that you ask enough questions to identify all the fees. In addition to these normal fees, some funds have additional fees, such as early redemption fees.

Dividend Income Is Subject to Income Tax

Dividend income is taxed at your income tax rate. When adding the highest federal tax bracket, 39.6%, to high local taxes, 6%, taxpayers in the highest tax bracket can lose 45.6% of their dividends to the annual income tax. Currently, the S&P 500 Index dividend payment is about 1.5%. Even if your dividends are reinvested in additional shares, the tax payments are due at year-end (unless you are investing in a tax-deferred IRA or 401(k) plan).

There is one way to eliminate the tax on dividend income, which we will discuss in Chapter 16, "Tax Strategies." If you incur expenses in the course of earning dividend income, such as margin interest, then the expenses are deducted from the income before the tax is calculated. If the expenses exceed the dividend income, then no dividend income tax is due.

Capital Gains Distributions

Mutual funds realize capital gains by buying and selling securities in the portfolio. The tax code requires that these taxable gains be distributed to fund shareholders by year-end. Short-term gains, less than twelve months, are taxed at your federal income tax rate plus your state income tax rate. Long-term gains, over twelve months, are taxed federally at 20% of the gain. (Some states tax long-term capital gains at the state income tax rate.) As a mutual fund shareholder you have to pay capital gains taxes on these capital gains dividends.

Most actively managed funds are managed to achieve the highest total return for their investors. The active trading that fund managers engage in trying to beat the competition realizes many gains. How much does it cost?

363 Equity Mutual Funds, 10-Year Total Returns (ending 12/31/1999)			
	Active Funds	Index Funds	Return Advantage
Pre-tax returns (after mgmt. expenses)	15.78%	18.10%	2.32%
After-tax returns (after mgmt. expenses)	13.39%	17.10%	3.71%
Cost of Taxes	2.39%	1.00%	-1.39%

We see in this spreadsheet that before-taxes index funds outperformed the average equity mutual fund by 2.32%. But after-taxes index funds outperformed active funds by 3.71%. The additional 1.39% return improvement came from the tax efficiency of index funds. (The income tax rate used in these calculations was 31%. All capital gains were assumed to be long-term and taxed at 20%. State taxes were not included. Your tax rates may be higher.)

But you may say, "Those are high returns (18%); what if the returns are lower?" If the total returns are lower, then saving 1.39% in annual taxes is more significant.

Successful Investing Taxes

In addition to annual taxes on dividends and capital gains distributions, investors must pay capital gains taxes on successful investing. If you buy a stock or mutual fund for $10,000 and you sell it when it has reached $20,000, you owe a 20% federal tax on the $10,000 long-term capital gain, plus any state tax. You could remain invested in an active fund for years without trading, but the likelihood of that is small. But index investors have no reason to trade their index funds. How much would we save by not trading and therefore deferring the long-term capital gains tax?

The Capital Gains Trading Spreadsheet shows three scenarios. In each case the portfolio doubles every five years. The first scenario, Never Trade, is to invest and never trade, which yields a 14.88% total return.

Never Trade	Start	5 years	10 years	15 years	20 years
Index	$10,000	$20,000	$40,000	$80,000	$160,000
Total Return			14.88%	14.88%	
10-Year Trades	$10,000	$20,000	$40,000	$68,000	$136,000
20% C.G. tax			$6,000		$20,400
Reinvest			$34,000		$115,600
Total Return			13.01%		13.01%
5-Year Trades	$10,000	$20,000	$36,000	$64,800	$116,640
20% C.G. tax		$2,000	$3,600	$6,480	$11,664
Reinvest		$18,000	$32,400	$58,320	$104,976
Total Return		12.48%	12.48%	12.48%	12.48%

In the second scenario, 10-Year Trades, we do a trade every ten years, and then deduct the tax and reinvest the rest to double every five years. Trading once every ten years reduces our rate of return to 13.01%.

The third scenario, 5-Year Trades, is to trade every five years. As before, we calculate the tax, deduct it, and reinvest the rest. This reduces our rate of return to 12.48%.

Trading once every five years cost us 2.40% of our total return (14.88%–12.48%). Trading once every ten years cost us 1.87%. Also notice that after twenty years the balance for the 'Never Trade' scenario was $160,000, while the '5-Year Trades' scenario has a balance of $104,976.

But you may say, "What if the market does not double every five years?" The 20% tax on our gains has the same effect whether gains are large or small. The advantage from not trading remains constant regardless of the level of returns.

Another person may object, saying, "The never trade scenario is not possible; you will have to spend your money sometime." Actually, if you leave the index funds to your heirs, the original cost basis is forgotten, and the shares pass at market value. Warren Buffett calls this strategy "buy and die." We will also examine other ways to defer, reduce, or avoid these taxes in a future chapter.

Summary of Benefits

We saved in management fees. We saved in annual taxes by being tax efficient. We saved from not trading and from deferring long-term capital gains taxes. These savings benefits are ours without our even considering that index funds outperformed the average active equity fund. And these savings are constant whether the market rises or falls. If the market earns a low return, saving on taxes and fees becomes even more significant.

In the next graph we did not use averages. These are the ten-year total returns on 363 equity mutual funds. The second graph is the ten-year total returns after expenses, loads, annual taxes, and the 2.40% tax cost of trading once every five years. In each chart the index funds are the vertical line in the middle, and we applied the same expenses, loads, and annual taxes, but not the 2.40% cost of trading once every five years.

Note that S&P 500 Index funds do better than the average equity fund in the top graph. But, in the bottom graph, which displays the total returns after all taxes and expenses are paid, the index funds beat nearly every equity mutual fund. For investors who pay taxes, the second graph is the one that matters.

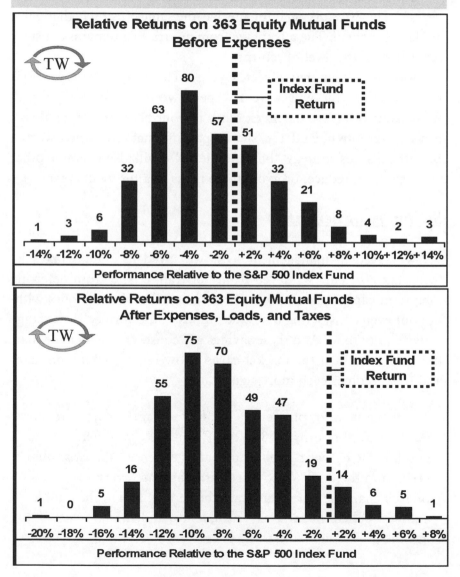

Here the results are summarized in a table. Using total returns before costs, the numbers that you read in the newspaper, the S&P 500 Index beat 67% of all equity mutual funds over this ten-year period (ending 12/31/1999). But after all the costs of investing are deducted, from the active funds and from the index funds, the index funds beat 93% of all the equity mutual funds.

Index Funds vs. 363 Equity Mutual Funds, 10-Year Total Returns
(ending 12/31/99)

	Below the Index	Above the Index	Index Beat
Before Costs	242	121	67%
After Costs	337	26	93%

---

441 Equity Mutual Funds, 10-Year Total Returns (ending 12/31/99)

	Active Funds	Index Fund	Advantage
Total Returns	16.83%	18.28%	1.45%
Returns after Costs	10.46%	17.10%	6.64%
Total Costs	6.37%	1.18%	-4.19%

On average the S&P 500 Index returned 1.45% more than the average active equity fund. But after all the costs of investing are deducted, the S&P 500 Index fund returned 6.64% more than the average active equity fund. This demonstrated extra 4.19% is a result of the low fees and low taxes that are associated with index investing. It is significant to note that the cost savings are a "constant" advantage; that is, these costs do not vary with the returns earned by the market. These cost savings apply whether returns are high or low.

Why Not Buy the Leaders?

After looking at this data some people might ask, "Why not just invest with one of the twenty-six funds that beat the market?" The funds that beat the market in this ten-year interval will probably not be the leaders in another ten-year interval because most of the top performers only have one or two great years. The rest of the time (years) they have average results. Over the long haul, this rotation of the leaders causes all mutual fund returns to approach the average return for the group. You will be interested to know that we can profit from this observation.

The returns on all equity mutual funds will approach the average as we invest for longer time periods. The longer the time period, the more the return on one active fund will approach the average return of all active funds. For example, the returns from these 363 active mutual funds for the past year were quite varied; the lowest fund return was –16.5% and the highest fund return was +182.5%. The returns for the past five years were less varied, –6.4% to +45.2%, the ten-year returns less varied still: –1.2% to +30.2% with the average at 15.78%. Longer time periods will produce a tighter distribution of returns for equity mutual funds. Therefore, if we beat 93% of all equity mutual funds with a ten-year investment horizon, we expect to beat an even greater percentage when we use a longer investment horizon.

Conservative Results

These are conservative results; the advantage of index funds over actively managed equity funds is understated for several reasons. For instance, there is a positive survivorship bias in the average ten-year returns of these 363 existing equity mutual funds. The 363 equity mutual funds are the survivors. That simply means that the really bad funds are not included in the results because they did not survive. If all funds that were in existence ten years ago but have since failed were included, the average equity fund would have earned 1.50% less.[1] In real life, any investor who selects a mutual fund has a chance of buying a fund that will do so badly that it will be closed or merged with another fund.

In addition, the tax rates that were used for these calculations assumed that all capital gains distributions were long-term capital gains taxed at 20%. And the income tax rate used was 31%. In your personal taxes, you will need to pay your income tax rate on short-term gains. In addition you will pay state taxes. Therefore, these after-tax returns understate the full cost of taxes, especially if your income tax rate is above 31%. For individuals in the higher tax brackets, this understatement will add another 1%.

Summary of Savings

In summary, we know that the market averages outperform the average investment manager. We used equity mutual funds as a proxy for all equity portfolios, and it would seem that equity mutual funds are in general well managed. But after paying expenses and taxes, the average S&P 500 Index fund outperformed all (93%) of the equity mutual funds. In addition, we expect that longer investment periods (fifteen years, twenty years, etc.) would improve this advantage. In addition, selecting an actively managed mutual fund is a game of chance, while selecting an S&P 500 Index fund involves no uncertainty.

In conservative round numbers, the index fund advantage consists of:

Index funds over average equity managers	+2.00%
Savings in expenses and taxes	+4.50%
Total savings	+6.50%

Total Wealth

To this 6½% advantage from index investing, we will add the advantage of living the endowment lifestyle and other sundry advantages along the way. You will be happy to know that the rest of this book will outperform what we have described so far.

CHAPTER 4

Historical Stock Returns

THE FIRST QUESTION THAT PEOPLE ASK is generally, "What if the market does not keep going up?" The more sophisticated ask, "What if the market does not keep going up at the present rate?" There is a two-part reply. First, we cannot promise that the market will go up with absolute certainty. But the second answer is, we can look at history and form an educated opinion about the historical nature of investment returns. If we believe that history will repeat itself during our lifetime, then we conclude that the market is very likely to continue going up. And we can form an opinion about the rate of return that we are likely to see.

Return Since 1802

This graph from the book *Stocks for the Long Run*[1] by Jeremy Siegel shows that stocks outperformed bonds and treasury bills from 1802 to 1997. Two hundred years of returns also show that stocks consistently outperformed bonds and bills over longer investment horizons. But, we can also see from the graph that the stock line is wigglier than the bond line or the bill line. That means that stocks are more volatile, and, therefore stocks may go down for short periods,

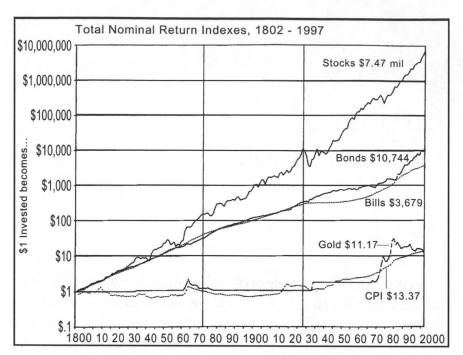

Total Nominal Return Indexes, 1802 - 1997

Jeremy Siegel, *Stocks for the Long Run*, 1998, McGraw Hill (reproduced with permission).

while bonds and bills are less volatile. Therefore, there are many short periods of time when bonds and bills returned more than stocks because, when stocks went down, bonds and bills held their consistent (but lower) average returns. We want to earn the high returns from stocks, but we also want the consistency (low volatility) of bonds and bills. By reading this book you will learn how to capture those higher long-term stock returns safely.

Since we are considering an index fund, which is compounding tax deferred, we need mentally to modify this graph. Using our strategy, we get to accumulate returns in our PEA at the stock rate. But if we put our money into bonds or bills we have to deduct the cost of annual taxes on those returns because interest income is taxed every year.

The compound rate of return for stocks over the entire period 1802 to 1997 is 8.4%.[2] The return for bonds for the period was

4.80% and the return for short-term government bills, was 4.30%. But we need to adjust these numbers by our after-tax rate. If we can capture compound returns from the stock market and defer the taxes on our gains to some distant date, the numbers look like this:

Returns 1802–1997	Stocks	Bonds	Bills
Pre-tax rate	8.40%	4.80%	4.30%
After-tax rate (40%)	8.40%–?%	2.88%	2.58%

Clearly, the effect of paying taxes today has a negative effect. With our PEA invested in index funds, we will not eliminate taxes. But we defer the taxes as long as possible, and during that time we accumulate compound returns at the stock rate. Also, we will examine strategies to reduce or avoid those deferred taxes. In addition, we will present strategies to benefit from our personal wealth without selling our index funds, thereby enjoying an endowed lifestyle while still invested. Finally, if you hold a portfolio until you die, the capital gains tax will never be paid. The assets will pass to your heirs at market value, and the original cost basis is forgotten. In short, paying the tax on interest each year instantly reduces your compound returns, but deferring the tax is beneficial. Therefore, when we consider the above graph of stocks outperforming bonds and bills, we need to remember that our strategy effectively increases the advantage of stocks over bonds and bills. Because we cannot predict the present effect of taxes that you may or may not pay in the distant future, the after-tax stock return has been filled with 8.40%–?.

Moreover, after noting that stocks have significantly and consistently outperformed bonds and bills since 1802, we see another interesting trend in this data. The market has been earning more than an 8.04% return recently, as we discussed in Chapter 1. The stock returns from 1946 to 1997 have been 12.20%, and from 1982–1997 stock returns have been 16.07%.[3]

Returns 1946–1997	Stocks	Bonds	Bills
Pre-tax rate	12.20%	6.10%	4.90%
After-tax rate (40%)	12.20%–?%	3.66%	2.94%

Stocks, bonds, and bills all earned higher returns in the last fifty years than over the past two hundred. And during the past fifteen years, the returns were higher still. In conclusion, stocks always outperformed bonds and bills, and the returns on stocks, bonds, and bills have been increasing through time.

Returns 1982–1997	Stocks	Bonds	Bills
Pre-tax rate	16.70%	8.70%	6.50%
After-tax rate (40%)	16.70%–?%	5.22%	3.90%

What Is Long Term to You?

In order to capture long-term stock returns, we need to stay invested for a long term. Time is the one commodity that costs us nothing, is equally distributed to all, and cannot be traded. Albert Einstein said, "Compound interest is the greatest mathematical discovery of all time." Do you think that is an exaggeration? We must all understand that compounding your returns is where the big money is. But compound returns require time.

Peter Minuit

It has been said that if the $24 that was paid to the Indians for Manhattan by Peter Minuit were compounded at 8%, it would be worth more than Manhattan today. Let's run the numbers. Peter bought Manhattan in 1620, 380 years ago. At 8% money doubles every nine years, and there are forty-two nine-year periods in 380 years. Thus, $24 times two raised to the forty-second power is $105 trillion. That certainly seems to be worth more than Manhattan, but let us do the math. Manhattan is approximately 200 blocks north to south and 10 blocks east to west, or 2,000 city blocks. $105 trillion divided by 2,000 blocks is $1.025 billion per city block. The average city block in Manhattan could be bought for much less than one billion dollars; therefore, Peter paid a fair price for Manhattan. Imagine how much you could accumulate if you could live four hundred years.

Life Expectancy

Medical science has increased the life expectancy of most people so much that we should reevaluate what constitutes long term. The oldest money managers alive today began their careers in the 1920s and 1930s. At that time people did not generally expect to live to be eighty or ninety or one hundred. Today many people do live that long. The U.S. Census Bureau predicts that there will be eight times as many centenarians in 2050 as there are today. Looking forward, we can predict that many people that are thirty years old today will exceed one hundred years. That gives today's thirty-year-old an investment horizon of seventy years. Someone who is born today should expect to live over one hundred years and therefore have a potential investment horizon of one hundred years.

Your Future Is Your Capital

With all the money that is spent by forecasters trying to predict the future of securities prices (and even then failing to significantly outperform the market averages), one has to wonder if more effort should be directed at predicting our own lives. Money, after all, is only a means to an end. The person who possesses the money is the one who benefits. Why don't we spend more time predicting our personal future? If you knew what you would want in the next few years, you could start planning now to obtain it.

Think of your future earnings as human capital. People will convert their wealth in the form of human capital into financial wealth by earning income, then saving and investing in financial assets.

It certainly seems as easy to predict the next major event in the life of an individual as to predict the next recession. Is it easier to predict your future salary than the earnings per share of IBM? Simply expecting the major events of your life, and planning now to achieve them, will significantly increase your success. Then you can optimize your present lifestyle to achieve what you will need in the future.

The point is, we need to optimize both income and outgo; but traditionally investment analysis has focused only on maximizing income and assumed that spending was someone else's problem. We are not limited to maximizing income only; we will also try to retain income as long as possible and maximize the benefits of having wealth.

Conclusion

Because rates of return have been increasing and because people are living longer, and because index funds are outperforming all other alternatives on an after-tax basis, it is time to reconsider the whole picture. We will find that we can put the pieces together to achieve a superior lifestyle for the individual. Would improving your lifestyle be something that you would care to consider?

CHAPTER 5
What Are Your Goals?

CAN YOU BEAT THE MARKET TOMORROW? No. Can you make a reasonable return that will support you in future years? Yes. But what is your goal in reading this? Do you want to speculate, risk your money, live dangerously, or bet the farm? We won't show you how to do that. We will show you how to achieve superior returns without risk.

We are going to demonstrate a tested method of safely achieving personal wealth while maintaining a lifestyle above your personal expectations. How can I say "above your personal expectations"? Most people have never imagined that they could live like this. Next you'll want to know, "What's the catch?" If there is a catch, it is "What are your goals, and is your behavior in line with your goals?"

Surprisingly, many people want to speculate. They are disappointed to learn that they can earn more money by not taking chances. Therefore, we will start with the first principle of investing: "Know your client." It may be you, or it may be someone for whom you are managing money, such as your parents or your children.

Suitability

Many people do not know that every registered securities salesperson must pass the National Association of Securities Dealers (NASD) examination, which means that all securities salespersons understand the principle called *suitability*. One of the guiding principles of securities sales is suitability, which means selling suitable investments to each investor. If your grandmother has no job and lives off the income from her investments, it is unsuitable to put all her money into securities which could decline significantly in value. For example, if she needs money for an emergency, she might be forced to sell securities at a loss. If a securities salesperson invests all her money in a single common stock, and she suffers a loss, she can take that salesperson to court and claim that she was sold unsuitable investments, and she'll win. It is the responsibility of the securities salesperson to know the client and what investments are suitable for that client.

Stages of Life

Therefore, you must know what your goals are. There are five main stages in life which directly influence your goals.

Youth

As a child you are dependent upon your family for support, education, and training. You have forty-five years of future earnings ahead of you before retirement, but you earn nothing at the present. If you have money and lose it, you cannot gain it back until you begin to work.

Young Adult

In your early adult years, you typically can earn your living but have little extra money. Therefore, you can tolerate some risk because, if you lose small amounts of money, you can earn more money. Also, you have twenty-five to thirty-five years before retirement.

Middle Age

In middle age people raise their children, buy a house, and pay for college, all major expenses which they can anticipate with reasonable certainty. They still have ten or twenty earning years until retirement.

Empty Nest

After people's children move out of the house, they are typically earning their peak salaries, their expenses decline, but they have only a few years before retirement. Therefore, they usually focus on accumulating capital to help them live comfortably in retirement. They may have only five to ten years until they retire.

Retirement

Once retired, people derive their name from Social Security and savings. There is normally no source of earned income; therefore, all expenses reduce savings. They still have ten to twenty-five years to live on their investments.

Investment Classes

There are four major classes of investments. Each is appropriate for different investment goals.

Savings

Savings accounts earn interest, are always available, and do not go up or down in value. FDIC insured savings accounts are insured by the federal government up to $100,000 even if the bank fails, but earn low rates of interest. Bank certificates of deposit are FDIC insured, have a fixed term, and earn a higher rate of interest. Treasury bills are issued by the U.S. government and have a fixed term of three, six, or twelve months. Money market funds are always available, like savings accounts, yet they earn higher rates of interest, but they are not insured. The money market fund buys bank CDs, treasury bills, and short-term corporate securities. If the money market fund invests in companies that go bankrupt, your money might not earn a high return or your principle might be at risk.

Fixed Income Investments

Fixed income investments, such as government bonds, corporate bonds, tax-free municipal bonds, and mortgages pay a fixed or floating rate of interest. While the principle may go up or down slightly, if held to maturity, you get all your money with interest. They are not insured, but investors can select fixed income investments with high credit ratings.

Preferred stocks pay a fixed dividend. That places them between bonds and stocks. There is some risk if the company fails, but generally they hold their value if the company remains in business. However, they will not appreciate if the company does well.

Equities

Stocks represent ownership in a business, and stocks can go up or down indefinitely. That means they can go to zero if the company fails. Or if the company does well, the stock will generally rise, sometimes dramatically.

Derivatives

Finally, there are derivative securities such as option contracts, warrants, rights, commodity and currency contracts, and many more. These securities are highly speculative, and they often expire after a fixed period of time. Frequently, when they expire they are worthless. Therefore, these investments are very risky.

In this category you should also include any investments that you do not understand. Not understanding what you are doing is beyond speculation.

If you are reading this to understand investing, that is a start. This brief overview of the different types of securities is not sufficient, and you should read a basic book on securities. There is a suggested reading list in Appendix A. Even though you may never buy some of these securities, it is very helpful to know what they are and to understand why the securities that you have chosen are correct for your investment goals.

Mutual Funds

Mutual funds are collections of any of the above securities. By owning a professionally managed collection of securities the investor gains three important benefits.

Diversification

One benefit is diversification, which means if the fund owns one hundred stocks and one goes bankrupt, it only hurts each investor in the fund 1%, as opposed to the individual who might invest all in one stock, have it fall to zero, and lose it all.

Professional Management

The second benefit is professional management. The fund management team makes a career of managing investments and therefore has an advantage over a less informed individual who may have less time to devote to the task.

Accountability

The third advantage is accountability. The fund results are published publicly, and an investor can see the manager's track record, as opposed to private investment counselors who do not have published track records. Frequently, private investment counselors claim that they are better than everyone else, but where is their evidence?

How Do You Select Suitable Investments?

What is the link between these investment types and the stages of your life? It is *time* and *risk*. How much time until you need the money? When you need the money determines how much risk you can take. Also, there are two time/risk horizons to manage—one is the risks in your investment portfolio, and the other is the risks in your lifestyle.

If you have an old car and only $500 in savings, you might need that money any day because you never know when the car will need repairs. Therefore, your time horizon should be tomorrow. Only a savings account or a money market account is suitable to cover your risk of suddenly needing the money. In other words, the old car is a risk in your lifestyle, but you can mitigate that risk by keeping your $500 in the savings account.

If you have a good job that covers your monthly expenses, your bills are paid, you have a healthy balance in your checking account and no pending expenses, and you have $10,000 in savings, then you might not need that money for some time. Depending on your stage in life, you could decide between stocks or fixed income investments as suitable investment vehicles. Here we have an individual with low lifestyle risk who can now consider investing in riskier investments to earn a higher rate of return.

But most people have both situations in their life at the same time. The realistic approach is that you need two accounts, a savings account for unexpected expenses like car repairs, and an investment account where you put money for the long term.

In summary, suitability consists in knowing which investments are suitable for which investors at which time during their life. The key variables are time and risk. When will they need their money back, and how much risk can they assume? In addition, present *income* and total *assets* are contributing factors. If you have a large income or a large endowment, then you can take on larger risks.

This ends our discussion of suitability. Suitability is the foundation of all investment decisions.

If you manage your investments, or someone else's investments, then you have made the suitability decision—because time is the key variable and time marches on no matter what you decide to do. Not having an investment strategy and not putting it into practice is a choice. Let me repeat that: if you are alive, you have already made a choice about managing your investments because you only have today once. What you neglect to do today, you cannot do tomorrow.

Asset Allocation

The next major principle of investing is asset allocation. We briefly mentioned having two accounts. Now that we have two accounts, we have to decide how much to put into each account, and what to put into each account.

Each person or family is different, and needs will change at different stages in life. Losing your job is generally the major risk for most breadwinners, and you should desire a savings account that can cover the amount of time that you might expect to be unemployed. If your spouse works, that amount might be less than if you are the sole source of income for a family with dependents.

If you do not have a supply of savings in a liquid account, experience has shown that something will go wrong, and you will then be forced to take the money in your investment account to cover the present emergency. This could cost you a lot in future dollars, as will be shown in the next sections. At this point we will postulate that your long-term investments will earn more if left undisturbed. You will always have unexpected expenses. Therefore, you need at least two types of assets: liquid savings and long-term investments. Some people may want to hold several types of assets. This is called asset allocation.

Under the category of liquid savings, we group all the accounts necessary for managing your daily life. Checking accounts, savings accounts, and credit card accounts. This includes savings for near-term major expenses.

Under the category of retirement accounts you might have an IRA, a Roth IRA, a 401(k), and a taxable PEA.

The question of how much to allocate to each class of assets should again be determined by when you will need the money and how much risk you can bear. But whatever you do with your money, you have allocated your assets. Our point is that you should decide what is the optimal asset allocation using these principles.

If you like to "play the market," you may want to have three accounts: a savings account where you save for purchases and to cover unexpected expenses, a PEA which you leave undisturbed for life, and a stock speculating account with which you "play the market."

If you are a philanthropist, you may have a separate account for charitable contributions, which will be disbursed in the near term but are kept separate from the household bills.

If you are saving for a near-term purchase, it is not suitable to put that money in the stock market because the market could go down over the short-time horizon. But you may be able to earn more than a money market rate by purchasing short-term bonds while you save for this future purchase.

This covers asset allocation. It is an enabling part of our investment strategy. In order to capture long-term stock returns, we need to allocate long-term funds to our Personal Endowment Account. We have to continue to operate our daily life and achieve our short-term goals using separate savings, checking, and credit card accounts.

Borrowed Money, or Leverage

In addition to earning and saving and investing money, you may consider borrowing money. Repaying debts generally requires a monthly income, which most people acquire by working. Therefore, borrowing money implies that you will continue working until the debt is repaid. In addition, the amount of monthly income available for debt repayment limits the amount a person can borrow.

Generally, people who are not working fall into two groups. Young people who have not yet begun to raise a family often interrupt working to travel or pursue interests such as surfing, skiing, music, and so on. And older people retire and live on their accumulated savings and social security/pensions. Both groups like to select locations where living expenses are low, since they wish to conserve their money and have little current income. Both groups are typically not supporting dependents.

People who are working, and expect to continue working, are not limited by manageable debts. For instance, houses may cost more in a metropolitan area, but there are more good jobs. Therefore, people who are working view the high cost of houses as a smaller obstacle than someone without a job.

When it comes to borrowing, the first consideration is your job and your commitment to continue working. If your goal is not to work, then borrowing is not for you, and any debts should be repaid. If you are going to continue working, then borrowing is limited by your income.

Collateral

Collateral differentiates loans. A loan against a house is a secured loan. If you lose the ability to repay the loan, you can always sell the house and pay off the loan. A car loan is similar. But a loan against your name only has no associated collateral. If you lose your ability to repay, where would you obtain the money to close the debt? An example of an unsecured debt would be a credit card loan. Therefore, we can differentiate between loans by looking at the collateral.

Lifestyle Options

You can consider your lifestyle choices as options. You may decide that you desire the freedom to live without working, and you keep your option to borrow. Or you may be in the process of raising a family, and therefore you are going to be working anyway, so you may trade your option to borrow for a mortgage on a bigger house. When it comes time to retire, you will not want to be repaying debts. Or if you want to start a business, you may wish to be free to earn subsistence wages for a few years. Owning your options gives you the freedom to leave your steady job.

In this simple example, we have uncovered a big investment principle. Choices are worth money. We will demonstrate this again in future chapters. Knowing what you want and what you will want in the future brings benefits, because lifestyle options can be traded for real value.

Goal Summary

We have outlined how your goals affect your investments. The key variables are time and risk and income. Money is your servant; use it to attain your goals. Knowing what your goals are is step one. Often we have goals, but our investment choices contradict what we really want. Let us postulate that goals come before investments. First, know what you want; then select investments that agree with your goals.

CHAPTER 6
The Endowment Lifestyle

WE HAVE ALREADY MENTIONED that one dollar becomes $64 in thirty years. But five years after that it doubles to $128, and then in five more years to $256, and so on. The hard part is the first thirty years and the first few dollars.

Just yesterday someone told me that her daughter had been advised to invest $166 per month between age twenty and thirty, and the result would be a fortune when she was ready to retire. Unfortunately, the next sentence I heard was, "But where is she going to get the money?" What is needed here is a change of lifestyle. This young person does not think getting old is something to get motivated about. I agree; it is hard to get worked up about retirement when you are twenty years old.

Plant a Seed

But a million dollars I can relate to! Therefore, let us rephrase this. Would you like to plant a seed that will grow into a fortune in your lifetime? Of course you would. And the more you spend on the seed, the bigger your fortune will grow.

Reap a Harvest

Second, when can I start to reap this harvest? There are two answers. One answer is never (but don't stop reading until you have heard the second answer). We said that you couldn't have your cake and eat it too. In other words, you either plant your seed or you spend it. If you want one dollar to grow to $64 or $128 or $256, then you can't spend it, it must stay invested for thirty years and then some more.

Here is the second answer: You can lend yourself money against your Personal Endowment Account. Let us say that you have been adding money to your PEA for a few years. Each year you drop in your tax refund, birthday presents, change that you collect on top of your dresser, year-end bonuses, and in addition the market has been good to you, and you have $20,000 in index funds. You are looking forward to having $80,000 in ten more years and $320,000 in twenty years. But now you need to buy a car and the average price of a car in your price range is $20,000. You could withdraw the money from your PEA and buy the car, but you think that in five years your car would be worth only $10,000, while the money would have doubled to $40,000 if left alone. Actually you expect to drive for at least fifty more years and the money would grow by 2^{10} which is $2,048,000—over two million dollars during your lifetime.

Chopping Down Your Cherry Tree

Now, when you look at it like that, you can see that taking the $20,000 out and buying the car is exactly what most normal people do. But you can also see that it is just like George Washington chopping down his father's cherry tree. For what reason did George chop down the cherry tree? It was to try out his new hatchet. You can understand why his father was angry. The only hope of benefit from that little cherry tree was that it would become a big cherry tree, and George's chopping it down killed that benefit. Moral of the story: Do not chop, uproot, defoliate, or kill your future benefits for a temporary gratification.

What can you do? Buy a used car, but this may not be an option for some people. What you can do is lease a car or borrow to purchase a car. That will leave your Personal Endowment Account intact. Each month the car payments will reduce what you might have added to your Personal Endowment Account, but they will preserve what you have already saved.

The Advantage of a Cash Lifestyle

An article in the *Christian Science Monitor* reported on a study of income, affluence, and lifestyle. The study compared people who buy things for cash to people who buy things on credit. It found that people who buy things for cash enjoyed a higher standard of living, an 8% better standard of living over the course of their lives. The people who bought for cash had to wait longer to purchase some possessions, but they did not have to pay any borrowing costs. Also, they were able to purchase bargains, whereas the borrowers often had to pay list price. How can we reconcile this with the above suggestion that you borrow to purchase a car?

Clearly the person who lives in debt is going to enjoy a lower standard of living than the person who saves and pays cash. Therefore, should we borrow to buy the car when we have the money?

The difference here is that you have enough money in your PEA to buy the car. But because that money is compounding at a target rate of 14.88%, doubling every five years, you have chosen to finance your car at 6% interest. You are not really a debtor, you are more like a banker borrowing at 6% and earning 14.88%. Therefore, do not think of yourself as a debtor; view your total net worth, which adds up to a positive number when you net out your assets and liabilities.

Now, borrowing money if you don't have a PEA is going in the opposite direction. Instead of a PEA that is accumulating compound interest, you are paying compound interest, and at the end of the year you have a depreciated asset to show for it. Let us do a spreadsheet. We will call the four plans the debtor, the buyer, the banker, and the saver.

Car Spreadsheet

	Debtor	Buyer	Banker	Saver
Starting PEA	$0	$20,000	$20,000	$20,000
Cost of Car	0	-20,000	0	0
Total Car Payments	-25,000	0	-25,000	0
Final Value of Car	10,000	10,000	10,000	0
Capital Gains Tax	0	-2,000	0	0
Growth in PEA	0	0	20,000	32,500
Total Profit/Loss	-$15,000	-$12,000	$5,000	$32,500
Deposits to PEA	$0	$0	$0	$25,000
Ending PEA	$0	$0	$40,000	$77,500

We see that the Debtor had the worst deal; he started with nothing, drove a car for five years, paid $25,000 in car payments, and ended up with a $10,000 car for a net cost of $15,000 and PEA of zero.

The Buyer started with $20,000 in his PEA, bought the car, and five years later it was worth $10,000 for a net cost of $10,000, which is better than the Debtor. In addition, if $10,000 of his PEA were a capital gain, then he owes the IRS 20% of $10,000 in tax at year end, or $2,000, making his true cost $12,000.

The Banker started with $20,000 in his PEA, borrowed to buy the car, paid $25,000 in car payments, and after five years the car was worth $10,000. But his PEA increased by $20,000, so he earned $5,000 while driving the car, and his PEA was preserved and stood at $40,000 after five years. Most important, the future value in his PEA continued to compound. Thirty years from now each dollar in the PEA will be multiplied by sixty-four (that is, $40,000 X 64 = $2,560,000).

Which lifestyle looks attractive now? And you do not have to wait until you retire to live like this. But don't get carried away and go lending yourself money to buy things without counting the cost. The last column in the spreadsheet is the Saver, who walked and ended up with $77,500 in the PEA. The thirty-year future value of walking for five years is $77,500 X 64 = $4,960,000.

But what about spendthrifts? There are a lot of us around. What hope is there for a normal person? The good news is that by financing the car our Banker was forced to mail a check each month for the car payment. This purchase created a disciplined savings program that probably exceeded what he would have saved on his own. Therefore, we see that by motivating the Banker to preserve his endowment, he increased his personal savings rate. To repeat that in plain English: some people need a kick in the pants to save money. If you need reminding, you can hire a bank to send you nasty reminders, and still drive a nice car.

This was a simplified example of buying a car. Appendix B, "Leasing or Buying a Car," goes into this subject in detail, but here is a thought for the present. Suppose that you own a car, and when its value declines to $10,000, you trade it for a new car. If you drive cars for fifty years, then you always have at least $10,000 worth of metal parked in your driveway. That is $10,000 that is not in your PEA. $10,000 compounding at 14⅞% for fifty years becomes $10,240,000.

Appreciating Assets

But we can do better than this. The car is a wasting asset. That simply means that its value goes down over time. The same is true for washing machines, furniture, stereos, and other appliances. What happens if we buy an asset that appreciates, like a house? Then the banker's plan of borrowing against the PEA looks even better because the value of the underlying asset is going up. Also, the IRS gives a tax deduction on interest paid on your house. Let's do the numbers again. But a house is a major investment, and most people do not have the full price; therefore, the decision is not to buy or borrow, but how much can I borrow. So we will add a new player to our spreadsheet, the homeowner.

House Spreadsheet

	Debtor	Buyer	Banker	Homeowner
Starting PEA	$0	$100,000	$100,000	$20,000
Cost of House	-10,000	-100,000	-10,000	-10,000
10 Years of Mtg. Payments	-72,000	0	-72,000	-72,000
Final Value of House	150,000	150,000	150,000	150,000
Loan Balance Due to Bank	-84,000	0	-84,000	-84,000
Capital Gains Tax	0	-16,000	0	0
IRS Interest Tax Credit	22,400	0	22,400	22,400
Growth in PEA	0	83,000	300,000	60,000
Total Profit	**$6,400**	**$117,000**	**$306,400**	**$66,400**
Deposits to PEA	$0	$72,000	$0	$0
Ending PEA	**$0**	**$155,000**	**$400,000**	**$80,000**

The house costs $100,000, and each person owns it for ten years. During those ten years the house appreciates to $150,000, and the Personal Endowment Account doubles twice.

The Debtor must present a $10,000 deposit to get a mortgage. His payments are $7,200 per year, totaling $72,000 over ten years. After ten years he owes the bank $84,000 of the $100,000 that he borrowed. Also, he is in the 40% tax bracket and his mortgage interest payments are tax deductible; therefore, his taxes are reduced by $22,400. He profited $6,400 by living in a house for ten years; that is better than paying rent. His ending PEA is zero.

The Buyer actually has $100,000 in his PEA. He takes the money and pays cash for the house, which is worth $150,000 after ten years. If the cost basis of his PEA were $20,000 there would be an $80,000 capital gain when he sold the index funds, and at 20% the tax would be $16,000. We assume the Buyer puts $7,200 per year into his PEA, total $72,000, and the PEA grows by $83,000 during the ten years for an ending PEA of $155,000. However, if the Buyer had not been saving $600 per month, he would have wiped out his Personal Endowment Account and all the future value that it holds.

The Banker also has enough in his PEA to buy the house. He puts up a $10,000 down payment and then owes $7,200 a year in interest, $72,000 over ten years. He also is in the 40% tax bracket so he gets a $22,400 tax credit. His PEA started at $100,000 and doubled to $200,000 in five years, then doubled again to $400,000 during the second five years, an increase of $300,000. His total gain in wealth is $306,400, and his PEA is intact with an account value of $400,000.

The Homeowner does not have enough to buy the house outright. But he has a balance in his PEA of $20,000. He puts down $10,000 to buy the house, pays $72,000 in interest, gets the $22,400 tax credit, and after ten years he owes the bank $84,000 of his original loan. His PEA has doubled twice, first to $40,000, then to $80,000, an increase of $60,000. His profit on the house is $66,400, and after ten years his PEA is intact with a balance of $80,000.

All these Homeowners, except the Buyer, had to make a $10,000 down payment. That means that they each had to have a savings account in addition to their PEA. Remember asset allocation? Also, consider their investment horizon. While they were accumulating $10,000 in their savings account, they knew they would buy a house in the next few years. Therefore, it was not appropriate to keep that money in the stock market due to market risk. (We will say more about market risk in Chapter 9.)

The Buyer is actually the big loser. He only made a $117,000 profit compared to the Banker who made $306,400. The Homeowner is the most typical. His profit was larger than the Debtor, and he preserved his Personal Endowment Account. In fact, starting with $20,000, the Homeowner is catching up to the Buyer. The Buyer began with five times more than the Homeowner, but now the Buyer has less than twice the Homeowner.

Note that all four had to save or spend $7,200 per year, or $600 per month. Life was no easier or harder for each of the four. But how they fared was a result of their choices. Remember that your choices are worth real value.

Are There Any Limits?

These principles of investing are not new. The great universities and foundations and wealthy families of the twentieth century have been using these principles. Now you can use these principles.

The amount of money that you can put to work earning more money is limited by the size of your PEA. If your little apple tree produces one bushel of apples, you can start a few seedlings. But if your apple tree produces twelve bushels, then you can start many seedlings; you can invest in many projects.

Borrowing Limits

Is there any difference between borrowing to buy a house or borrowing to go on vacation, or something else? There is a big difference in the collateral value of the asset. We briefly mentioned wasting assets and appreciating assets. Let's list a few things that people use borrowed money to buy, in order of their lasting and appreciating (or depreciating) value. At the top of the list is a college education, a house, a car, a couch, a television, and a vacation, which comes at the bottom of our list. If you borrow to buy a house, you can always sell the house and repay the loan. If you borrow to go on vacation, there is no residual value after the vacation. Let's limit ourselves to purchasing assets that hold their value, at least until the loan is repaid. Why is this important? Because we are interested in making our total wealth grow, not shrink. If we sell all our assets and repay all our loans, we want to be sure that the remainder (the amount that belongs to us) is a positive number and growing. That is what total wealth is all about.

The first limiting factor is growth. We want our total wealth to increase.

What about buying a business? Is there a difference between borrowing to purchase a house and borrowing to start a car wash? The major difference is the risk. Usually, people live in their houses and insure their houses. There is little risk of losing a house. But when people borrow money for other projects, such as starting a business, the risk of losing the capital increases. The car wash may fail, but the loan will still need to be repaid. What would that do for our total wealth?

Is there a difference between obtaining a loan using your house as collateral and borrowing against your Personal Endowment

Account? Borrowing against the securities in your Personal Endowment Account is called margin borrowing. We will digress for a few moments to explain margin borrowing.

Margin Borrowing

The Federal Reserve Bank sets the rules governing margin accounts. Suitable investors may borrow up to 50% of the market value of approved securities in their margin account, putting their securities as collateral for the loan. For example, if you had a Personal Endowment Account with $100,000 in index funds, you could borrow another $100,000, and you would pay the brokerage firm interest on the loan. You could then buy $100,000 more of index funds so that your account has a total market value of $200,000. If your account doubles in five years, your market value would rise to $400,000; you would have paid $45,000 interest, and you would owe the brokerage firm its $100,000. Therefore, your final market value is $255,000 after five years instead of the $200,000 that you would have if your $100,000 had simply doubled to $200,000 in five years. This is called buying on margin.

But you should not do this because the stock market is volatile. The stock market could go down 25%; it could go down 30%. Let's say that you just margined your $100,000 account, borrowing $100,000, and bought $200,000 in index funds, and the market goes down by 33% in the next few weeks. Your account value is reduced by $66,000 to $134,000. In the eyes of your brokerage firm, you owe them $100,000, and you have $34,000 of equity in your margin account. Your equity to account value is 34%. At an equity to account value ratio of 35%, they will close you out, meaning they will sell your securities to cover the loan and return any leftover money to you. But before the account even gets close to

$135,000 (equity/loan = 35,000/100,000 = 35%), they will ask you for more money, known as a margin call. If you do not add more money to bring your equity in the account above 35%, they will sell your securities and return the remaining $34,000 to you. How do you feel about that? One day you had $100,000 and a few weeks later you have $34,000.

Even a minor downturn could become expensive. Suppose that you had $100,000 and borrowed $100,000 more on margin giving you a total account value of $200,000. If the market only declines 20%, your account value goes to $160,000. Your equity is $60,000, and your debt is $100,000.

Now, suppose that a lifestyle opportunity, or emergency, occurs, and you need the money. You would sell the securities for $160,000, pay off the loan, and you would have $60,000 left. And how do you feel about that? Your Personal Endowment Account was just cut from $100,000 to $60,000. Is that what you had in mind when you invested? What are your goals, and how much risk are you ready to take?

A second consideration is that speculative margin borrowing becomes addictive. If you do well, do not expect that after five years you will still have your original loan amount. People who margin their securities get addicted to that extra edge, and they keep increasing their borrowing as the market goes up. Therefore, whenever the market goes down, they are fully leveraged. If you like to sleep well at night, and if one of the benefits of investing in index funds is not having to watch your investments, then margin debt is not for you.

And don't think that you won't get to the same place. In our example above, the margin borrower ended up with $255,000 instead of $200,000 after five years. If you wait another eighteen months, you will arrive at the same place without taking the risk of cutting the value of your Personal Endowment Account.

Now back to the discussion of the endowment lifestyle.

Buying a Million-Dollar House

You can use your Personal Endowment Account to allow you to buy houses, invest in businesses, and undertake projects that will make you money in the future. The amount of borrowing that you can afford will increase as your PEA increases. If you have a $20,000 Personal Endowment Account, don't try to buy a million-dollar house—the interest would be $72,000 a year, or $360,000 over five years. But if you had $500,000 in your Personal Endowment Account, and you could pay $360,000 in interest over five years, your PEA would double to $1,000,000. On balance you would gain $140,000 before you even considered any increase in market value of the house. So the first limiting factor is profit. The homeowner with $500,000 in the PEA makes a profit while owning a million-dollar house, but the homeowner with $20,000 in the PEA loses money while owning the million-dollar house.

The second limiting factor is income. Can you pay the $72,000 per year interest cost?

The third limiting factor is lifestyle risk. Suppose two home-owners both earn $180,000 a year, or $15,000 a month. Both decide that they can pay the $6,000 monthly mortgage payment. Both buy a million-dollar house, and both go on a two-week vacation. When they return, they both learn that their company merged and their jobs have been eliminated. They are then both unemployed for six months. The one with a $20,000 Personal Endowment Account has to feed the family and can't make the mortgage payments. He loses the house and may end up bankrupt. The one with $500,000 in the PEA has no problem paying the bills. Besides losing money overall, the person with the $20,000 PEA took on too much risk, and when adverse circumstances arrived, he was wiped out. We all have lifestyle risks.

We know that you would never do this, but imagine for a moment how the man with the $500,000 PEA would feel if he had fully margined his PEA. How would he feel if he had margined his PEA and the market was down when he lost his job? Recessions, layoffs, and market declines frequently come together.

The Size of Your PEA

Increasing the size of your PEA increases the amount of money that you can borrow and still grow overall. Increasing the size of your PEA reduces your risk. The bigger your PEA, the bigger the lifestyle you can support. Have you ever wondered who owns those million-dollar condos in Miami Beach? People who can afford them probably own them. At the end of each year, the owners are worth more money, and despite the condo, their total wealth continues to increase.

Summary: Living an Endowed Lifestyle

So who thought that your Personal Endowment Account was only for retirement? Who thought a twenty-year-old would not be interested in a Personal Endowment Account? Who said, "You can't have your cake and eat it too"? We did. Let's just say our cake is doubling every five years, and we used that growth to borrow another; we are eating the cake of opportunity. How do we know when to stop? We don't want to start eating into our own cake. We don't even want to risk having to eat our own cake. If we invest in secure projects, those that have their own collateral, then we can use our PEA as an insurance policy against adverse circumstances.

Do you have a feel for the right balance between the size of your PEA and the amount of borrowing that you can afford? Do you see that paying cash for everything is better than going into debt, but that becoming a Banker is better still? The resources that we have been given are for us to use. Wisdom on how to use what we have been given is for us to seek. Please do not read this and then run out and buy something like an index fund. Read this and try to understand how it applies to your personal situation. Once you feel comfortable with where you are today, how these principles apply to you, and where you want to go—then run out and buy an index fund. The difference is that in the years to come, when your life and your goals have changed, if you understand what you are doing, you will be able to change your strategy to fit your changing goals.

The Endowment Lifestyle Will Improve Our Investment Results

Besides bringing benefits directly, the endowment lifestyle contributes to the income earned from index funds because it allows your PEA to compound undisturbed for your entire life. As we will see in future chapters, a long-term investment horizon reduces the risk of volatile stock returns. A long-term investment horizon defers long-term capital gain taxes, thus increasing your total return. Also, the endowment lifestyle protects your endowment. No matter what advances or reversals happen in your life, the endowment always grows, sometimes faster or sometimes slower, depending on what you can contribute, but it always grows by compounding. In addition, it provides a cushion against calamity. Finally, it is always easy to obtain credit. What bank would reject a loan applicant who had enough money to repay the loan?

Compared to a save-and-spend lifestyle, where you save to buy a car, then spend the savings and begin saving again, the endowment lifestyle accumulates wealth without interruption. This causes compounding to operate on a larger PEA balance. Imagine if all the cars you ever owned (or will own), plus your house, plus other major expenses were all in your PEA compounding for life. How large would the resulting PEA be?

But how much will you earn? In the following chapters we will discuss the rewards and the risks of investing. The market does not always go up. Your Personal Endowment Account does not always double on schedule. What kind of volatility can you expect, and what risks should you be prepared for? And what kind of rewards can you expect? What is the certainty of avoiding the risks and obtaining the rewards? The good news is you won't be disappointed. The endowment lifestyle opens the door to higher returns than many people have ever dreamed of earning.

Chapter 7

Financing a College Education

WE HAVE NOT EXHAUSTED THE CREATIVE WAYS in which you can harness the power of your Personal Endowment Account. Any time you are expected to spend a large amount of money, there is the possibility of using endowment power instead of cashing in your index funds. Paying for college is certainly a large expense.

Let's say that a family has saved the money to send a child to college. Should they consider borrowing to pay for college so that their savings can remain invested in an index fund to grow and support them in retirement? If they have a job and can borrow $100,000 at 7% and pay it back over ten or fifteen years, the $100,000 that is in their PEA would become $400,000 to $800,000. Is that a better way for the family to manage their college savings? Once you pay the tuition, you'll never see that money again.

Two Personal Endowment Accounts

But we could create two Personal Endowment Accounts. Suppose the student borrowed money to pay for college, and the parents put the money that they were planning to pay the college into an index fund for the student. The student now funds a PEA at a young age.

In this way two people create or preserve a PEA from the same college tuition, the parents and the student. The parents preserve their PEA and fund the start of a PEA for the student.

That was quick; let's restate the idea. The parents could pay for college from their PEA, but instead they elect to borrow the money and repay the loan from future income. This preserves their PEA, continues to defer the capital gains taxes, and their PEA will be larger when they retire. Also, the student has his own PEA that he has been funding with savings, gifts, and summer jobs. Now the parents decide that instead of paying the college tuition from the proceeds of their loan, they will put the money into the student's PEA. The student then takes out a college loan that pays the tuition. Therefore, two people, the parents and the student, preserve or create a Personal Endowment Account from one college tuition.

Of course, the downside is that the student now has a debt to pay, and so do the parents. But, this downside is mitigated by the fact that if necessary, they could sell the index funds to pay off the loan. (If the market had gone down, there might not be sufficient funds to fully pay off the loan.)

If the student understands the goals of this program, which we outline in this book, the student might want to create the debt and start life with a bigger PEA. Which would you choose?

More Ideas

This is not the last creative idea; the possibilities are endless. Whenever you are facing a large payment, ask yourself in advance, "How could I retain this wealth in my PEA?" The key is anticipating these expenses in advance, before the money is spent.

CHAPTER 8

Stock Market Indexes

To BEGIN WITH, Latin scholars will want to say "indices." Either spelling, indexes and indices, is recognized. Wall Street enthusiasts will often refer to "the stock market" when what they really mean is the Dow Jones Industrial Average or the Standard and Poor's 500 Index. When someone in America says, "The market went up last month," he is speaking of one of these two indexes.

We have briefly mentioned the S&P 500 Index (the S&P), and you are probably familiar with the Dow Jones Industrial Average (the Dow). The Dow Jones Industrial Average is an average of the stock prices of thirty industrial companies. Now, the thirty members' stocks change from time to time as companies prosper or decline. For example, the Dow used to contain railroad stocks, now this index contains airline stocks. If one company leaves the index, another is included.

The S&P is an index of the stocks of the leading 500 companies in the United States. To be included in the S&P 500 Index a company must be a leader in its market sector. The 500 leading companies are not necessarily the largest companies in the U.S. economy, but they comprise 69% of the total capital of all publicly traded U.S. companies.[1]

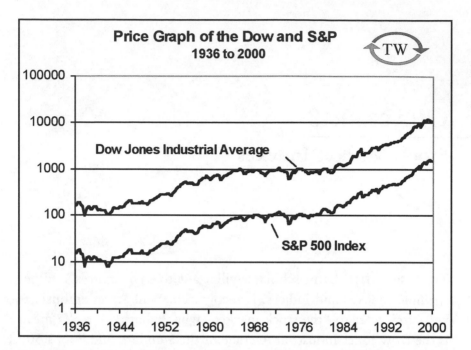

Amazingly, the Dow Jones Industrial Average and the S&P 500 Index have demonstrated very similar movements during the past fifty years (see graph). Most market participants prefer the S&P 500 as an index because it reflects the "broader market." To understand how thirty stocks and 500 stocks could move alike for over fifty years, you have to realize that stocks tend to go up and down together (except for the one that you own). Each stock may be independent, but the market acts like a school of fish or a herd of animals; all American stocks tend to travel together.

Note that this graph has a logarithmic scale, which is convenient when plotting price movements from ten to ten thousand. In a logarithmic graph, percent change is constant; each horizontal grid line on this graph represents a tenfold increase in value. The Dow moved from one hundred to ten thousand, while the S&P moved from fourteen to one thousand four hundred. This graph of price changes reveals a hundred-fold increase from the 1936 to 2000.

Both the Dow and the S&P show only price change. When a stockholder owns a stock, dividends are normally paid, and dividends increase the stockholder's total return. If the dividends are reinvested to purchase more shares, this causes compounding. Over time the market rises, and each quarter the investor purchases more shares with the dividends. Thus, the price is rising on a growing portfolio of shares.

Normally, the total return on the Dow and S&P indexes is not printed in the newspaper, because for a short term, less than a few years, the compounding effect is small. However, when considering long-term investments, the compounding becomes an important positive contribution. We will also look at price indexes to chart shorter-term market movements and at total return to compare long-term movements.

As long-term investors, we are interested in total return, which is much greater than simple price change because of the effect of compounding. For example, during the time period above, 1936 to 2000, the price of the S&P 500 increased about a hundred-fold. During the same period, one dollar invested in the S&P 500 became $1,397, a 1,397-fold total return.

CHAPTER 9

What Are the Risks?

Behavior, the Biggest Risk

THE SECURITIES MARKET IS THE RISK that most people focus on. But we are presenting a lifestyle approach to maximizing your personal wealth, which involves other risks. The main risk comes from your misbehaving. By misbehaving we mean, of course, that you do not behave in a manner that is consistent with your goals.

Personal House Buying Story

The second risk is that your life changes, therefore changing your long-term goals, but you make no adjustments to your investments. I'll tell you my story. I purchased a house and fixed it up with a gorgeous kitchen. It was in one of the better neighborhoods, and real estate prices had gone up due to high inflation in the eighties. I had no mortgage, and one day we decided to move; it was August 21, 1987. Our house sold quickly, and we selected a house to purchase that cost $50,000 more with a closing date of December 1987. Had my goals changed?

TOTAL WEALTH

I knew that my goals had changed. I was a cash buyer, and I had my long-term savings invested in the stock market. I planned to take the money that I needed out of the stock market and pay the difference on the two houses. What had changed? My time horizon had changed. In August 1987, I decided to buy a house in the near term. I knew that I should take my money out of the stock market, but the market was going up so nicely that I got greedy and decided to leave my money in stocks so that it would be worth more. Did I forget suitability? Looking back, August 21, 1987, was the market high. In October 1987, the market crashed 35%. When I closed on the house in December my securities were worth 30% less than when I counted my money in August. To complete the purchase of the house, I had to sell when the market was down. Some people would blame that on market risk. I think not; it was because my behavior was inconsistent with my goals. When the time horizon of my investments changed to several months, I should have withdrawn my money from the stock market.

If my time horizon had been several years, the crash would have been no problem. One year later the market was back up again, and in the ten years since the market has doubled several times. First, I took my money out of the market when it was down. Then I pouted for at least seven years and would not invest again because I was sure that there would be another crash. So first I lost money; then I failed to be in the market while it was going up. In fact, I lost more by staying out of the market. Finally, I paid cash for the new house. Now, I realize that I could have lived in the new house, left my principal in the market, and today I would be worth many times more. But let's move on to the future. The point to remember is that you are the one who has to manage your behavior. And behavior, which is contrary to your real goal, is the biggest risk.

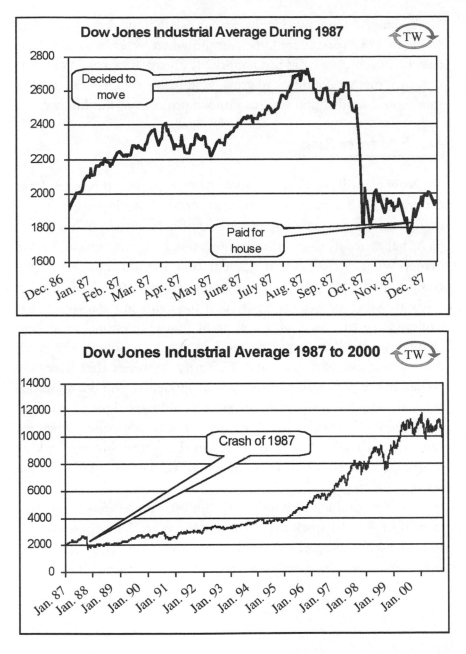

Looking at these two graphs, we can see that the drop that looked so big in 1987 (first graph), looks small when we look back in time (second graph). How did this happen? It always happens. As long as the stock market continues to grow, yesterday's problems always get smaller and smaller and smaller. Can we profit from this knowledge?

Stock Market Risk

Now we will consider the stock market. At least this is a risk we can measure. But most of the presentations of stock market graphs do not answer the most important questions, such as, "What would have happened to me? Exactly how much money would I have made? What is the greatest amount that I could have lost?" We could call the answers to these questions relevant stock market analysis. Much of what is reported in the daily and weekly news is irrelevant to the goals of a long-term index investor. In the next chapter we look at answering the important questions. The stock market may be risky, but we can identify strategies that have succeeded in the past. Using history as our guide, we will draw conclusions about what a successful investor could have done in the past. If the trends are broad based, consistent, and compelling, then we can expect to achieve similar results in the future. We are looking for long-term trends that have existed in the past and will continue into the future.

You are reading this book today. But our conclusions about how to profit from the stock market were true years ago. These conclusions are true now and will still be true years from today. The dates will change, but the conclusions remain constant over time.

CHAPTER 10

Minimizing Stock Market Risk

ON THE NEXT TWO PAGES, SEVEN GRAPHS COVERING the same time period are arranged to show how long-term investing minimizes market risk. The top graph is the price movements in the S&P 500 Index.

The next graph shows annual total returns on the S&P 500 Index from June 30, 1936, until September 29, 2000. Total return is different from price movement (top graph). Total return includes reinvesting dividends in the index. In the sixty-four years from 1936 to 2000, there are 258 quarters. In each quarter we invested for one year and plotted the total return. The result is the 254 one-year holding periods (vertical bars) shown on the graph. The lowest annual total return was –50%; the highest annual total return was +60%. The interesting thing about this graph is that it shows what an investment horizon of one year can give you—high volatility. There are many negative numbers, and if you had put money in the S&P 500 Index for one year, this is a picture of the variety of total returns you would have experienced over the past sixty-four years. On a positive note, notice that positive returns consistently outnumber negative returns, and the positive returns are on average larger than the negative returns.

TOTAL WEALTH

Graphs of Total Return Using Increasingly Longer Investment Periods

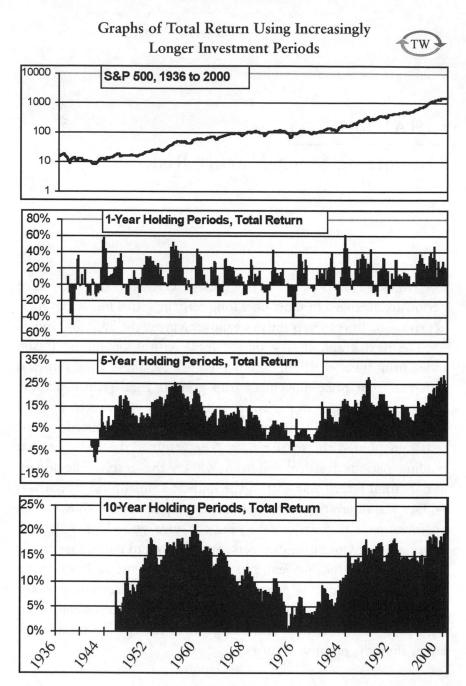

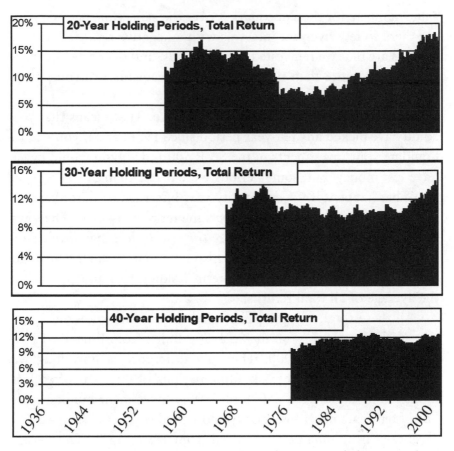

To construct the six total return graphs, we used the same data. Each quarter we bought the S&P 500 Index, and then we sold at the end of the holding period (one year, five years, etc.) and calculated our total return. We started a new investment each quarter, and we therefore have a rolling graph of returns on the S&P 500 for the period (one year, five years, etc.).

The third graph shows the results of five-year holding periods. When we look at the same S&P 500 total returns over five-year intervals, almost all returns are positive. Here we invested each quarter and stayed invested for five years, creating 198 five-year holding periods. What happened to the down years? These are the same numbers for the same market over the same time period. Why are there so few five-year intervals with a negative return? The two reasons are that we reinvested the dividends, and over time the market goes up more than down. The up movements overcome brief intervals of negative returns.

The ten-year total returns are all positive. That means that you could have picked any ten-year period since 1936, and if you had to liquidate your investments in the S&P 500 Index, you would never have lost money. But, some periods were better than others.

What happens if we use twenty-year intervals, or thirty-year, or forty-year intervals? The returns become more consistent. The lows go away. *Therefore, you can reduce the risk of loss significantly by staying invested for the long term.* Also note that the high returns go away. The total return over long-term holding periods approaches the average of all total returns.

All these total return graphs were drawn with the same data, that is, the total return on the S&P 500 Index from June 30, 1936, until September 29, 2000. The only difference is how long we stayed invested. Investment holding periods of one year often lost money and varied from –50% to +60%. Investment holding periods of ten years never lost money and varied from +0.5% to +20%. Twenty-year holding periods varied from 7% to 18%. Thirty-year holding periods varied from 9% to 14%. The forty-year holding periods were almost all between 11% and 13%. Now ask yourself, how long do I have to stay invested, or, when will I need to withdraw my money?

Have we promised what the next twenty years will bring? No, but based on the past sixty years we see a consistent trend. And this is the result of the top five hundred U.S. corporations, a group that may see membership changes but twenty years from now will still be the top five hundred U.S. corporations. Do you think that the top five hundred U.S. corporations will continue to perform better, worse, or the same for the next sixty years?

We showed these graphs to demonstrate that investing for the long term will minimize your risk of losing money. To review: If your investment horizon is one year or less, there is a significant chance of losing money. But if your investment horizon is five years, the risk of loss is reduced. And investment intervals of ten years or more never lost money. Also, as we invest over longer intervals, the returns become more consistent and less volatile, thereby reducing the risk of loss.

History Plus Common Sense

Considering these graphs of total return, could we have done better? The question we are going to pose, and then answer, is, "In the graph of ten-year returns, could we have removed the lowest returns by waiting until the market went back up?" First, we have to remember that each vertical bar represents a holding period return. A holding period return is simply the money that you invested (plus any reinvested dividends) evaluated on the day that you sell. We cannot change the day or price at which we invested, but we are in control of the day on which we sell. The lowest return, +0.5%, came from buying on September 30, 1964, and selling on September 30, 1974. There was a market low in the fall of 1974, with the Dow down 45%. It was a sale at this time that created the lowest ten-year total return between 1936 and 1998. We propose that we could raise our return by not selling at exactly ten years (when the market was down), but waiting until the market went back up. In the graph of ten-year returns, we added the white line, which shows how our strategy worked out. As you can see from the white line on the chart, if we have only invested long-term money in our PEA, we can "wait out" down markets and effectively avoid the worst returns.

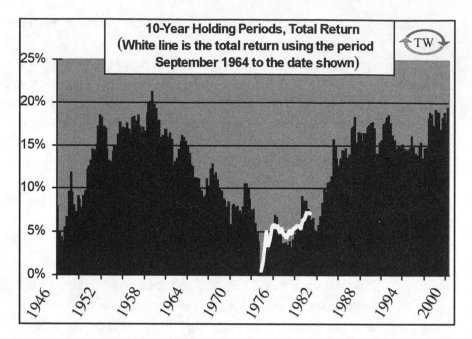

History tells us that the market goes back up; therefore, if we can wait out down markets, we can improve our total return. If we can delay our sale, then we can reasonably expect to avoid selling at the bottom of major down markets.

An Average of Averages

Using our strategy of investing in a market index and investing for a long term, we achieve average results in two ways. The market index gives us the average return across all stocks in the index. The long-term investment horizon gives us the average daily return over many days.

This also reduces our risk in two ways. The market index reduces our exposure to underperforming stocks. And the long-term investment horizon reduces our exposure to down days.

Dollar Cost Averaging

We can postulate a third strategy to avoid risk by looking at these results. In the data presented above, we invested all our money at the start and withdrew it all on the last day of the investment period. This is like investing all your savings on one day in a lump sum. Let's suppose that you have a large sum of money to put to work in the stock market. You are concerned that you will invest on a "high point" and that the market will then go down. We can avoid buying at the high by investing a portion of our money at regular intervals. If we divide our sum of money into three equal parts and invest once each month for three months, we would have an average cost. This will guarantee that we don't buy at the top. This technique is called "dollar cost averaging."

Dollar cost averaging is also good if you want to invest your savings each month. If you put a sum of money into the market each month for life, then you not only enjoy the benefits of index funds but you also know that you will not invest at the high, but at the average. Therefore, you reduce the problem of entering the market with a lump sum of money and then having the market go down.

Compare the two graphs on the next page. The top graph is the same graph of ten-year total returns on the S&P Index that we showed earlier. The lower graph used the same data but used dollar cost averaging. While similar, note that the extreme highs and lows have been removed from the second graph. This demonstrates the risk reduction that dollar cost averaging provides.

A second benefit of dollar cost averaging is that when the market goes down, your sum of money buys more shares. For example, suppose an investor buys two hundred shares at $10 ($20,000); then the price rises to $20, then falls to $5, and finally returns to $10. This investor will finish with the $20,000 that he started with. A second investor buys $10,000 when the price is $20 (fifty shares) and $10,000 when the price is $5 (two hundred shares), and at the

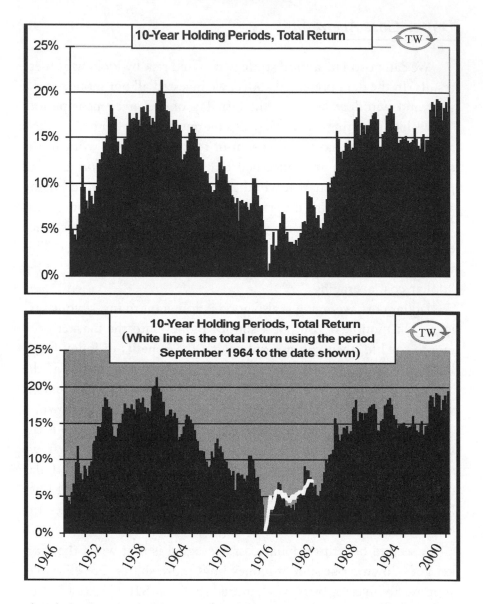

finish he has 250 shares at $10. The second investor finishes with $25,000. Dollar cost averaging increased the return of the second investor because he bought fewer shares when the price was high and more shares when the price was low. He also invested $20,000, but obtained 250 shares. Therefore, when markets go up and down, dollar cost averaging mathematically lowers your average cost, increasing your returns.

Conclusion

The volatility of the returns of the stock market (S&P 500) makes short-term investments very uncertain (read: big profits or big losses). But staying invested for a long term dramatically increases the certainty of receiving a sure return. Therefore, investors who stay invested for long terms eliminate the uncertainties of the stock market. In addition, dollar cost averaging further reduces the uncertainty of stock market returns. We have removed risk three ways by averaging. By investing in the index, we earn the market average and reduce exposure to underperforming stocks. By investing for a long term, we earn the long-term average and reduce exposure to down days. By dollar cost averaging, we invest at the average price and reduce exposure to buying high and selling low. In addition, we saw that if we are able to delay selling our investments, then we can wait out down markets and avoid low returns. Finally, this relevant research used the actual total return on the S&P 500 Index for the past sixty-four years.

We cannot promise that the future will be the same as the past, but using history as a guide we can confidently expect to reduce the risks of investing in the S&P 500 Index by remaining invested for a long term. And we can expect that the longer our investment horizon, the more certain our return will become. Thus we have demonstrated that investing for the long term in a market index will minimize stock market risk.

CHAPTER 11
Stock Market Volatility

How Deep Is a Dip?

WHILE INVESTORS WERE EARNING the long-term returns that we
showed in the last chapter, the market was going up and down daily.
The secret to living through the daily gyrations is having a historical
perspective of the market. What is a big decline? How long do big
declines last?

What should you be looking for in the table on the next page?
You should look for the worst declines that you might have to go
through if you are invested for the long term. Our definition of long-
term investing includes riding through the declines, not selling when
the market is down. Anyone can stay invested when his or her portfolio is growing, but a close inspection of this table reveals that the
market does not go up for any long term. Therefore, we can conclude that if you are a long-term investor, your long-term future will
include some significant market declines.

Dollar Cost Averaging

We already mentioned dollar cost averaging in the prior chapter.
We can postulate a risk-avoidance strategy for entering the market by

TOTAL WEALTH

High Date	Low Date	Max. Decline	Avg. Decline	Down Months	Recover Date	Up Months	Total Months
11/21/16	12/19/17	-40.1%	-28.0%	13.1	7/9/19	18.7	31.8
11/3/19	8/24/21	-46.6%	-31.1%	22.0	12/31/24	40.2	62.2
9/3/29	7/8/32	-89.2%	-67.9%	34.6	11/23/54	268.5	303.1
10/31/29	11/13/29	-27.4%	-20.7%	0.4	11/14/29	0.0	0.4
5/8/31	6/2/31	-21.2%	-18.6%	0.8	6/3/31	0.0	0.8
9/23/31	10/5/31	-25.4%	-21.3%	0.4	11/9/31	1.1	1.5
9/7/32	2/27/33	-37.2%	-25.5%	5.8	5/10/33	2.4	8.2
7/18/33	10/19/33	-22.4%	-19.2%	3.1	1/30/34	3.4	6.5
2/5/34	7/26/34	-22.8%	-20.2%	5.7	5/8/35	9.4	15.1
3/10/37	4/28/42	-52.2%	-33.3%	62.5	12/10/45	43.4	105.9
9/22/37	3/31/38	-37.2%	-27.1%	6.3	11/9/38	7.3	13.6
11/14/38	4/11/39	-20.5%	-18.5%	4.9	9/12/39	5.0	9.9
5/29/46	6/13/49	-24.0%	-19.9%	37.0	4/24/50	10.4	47.4
12/13/61	6/26/62	-27.1%	-22.9%	6.5	9/5/63	14.3	20.8
2/9/66	5/26/70	-36.6%	-27.9%	52.2	11/10/72	29.5	81.7
2/16/66	10/7/66	-24.2%	-19.7%	7.8	11/29/68	25.7	33.5
1/11/73	12/6/74	-45.1%	-33.4%	23.1	11/3/82	94.9	118.0
9/21/76	2/28/78	-26.9%	-21.7%	17.5	3/25/81	36.8	54.3
4/27/81	8/12/82	-24.1%	-19.9%	15.7	10/20/82	2.3	18.0
8/25/87	10/19/87	-36.1%	-31.6%	1.8	8/24/89	22.2	24.0
7/16/90	10/11/90	-21.2%	-19.2%	2.9	4/17/91	6.2	9.1
Averages		-33.7%	-26.1%	15.4		30.6	46.0
Averages without the Great Depression		-30.9%	-24.0%	14.5		18.7	33.1

Using the Dow Jones Industrial Average, from 1914 to 2000 there have been twenty-one declines exceeding 20%. In this table, the "Max. Decline" is the percent decline from the "High Date" to the "Low Date." The "Avg. Decline" is the average decline of all holding periods, which terminated on the Low Date. "Down Months" is the number of months between the "High Date" and the "Low Date."

The "Recover Date" is the date the Dow recovered its prior high; "Up Months" is the number of months from the Low Date to the Recover Date. "Total Months" is the total time from the High Date to the Recover Date.

looking at this data. Let's suppose you have a sum of money to put to work in the stock market. You are justifiably concerned that you might invest on one of these "high dates" and that the market will then go down. If you need your money short term, then you have a big problem. But if you paid attention to "suitability," your horizon is long term and you should weather the down market over time. But you will still suffer from having bought at the high. You can avoid buying at the high by investing a portion of your money at regular intervals, dollar cost averaging. With dollar cost averaging you invest the same amount of money at regular intervals. But you need to stick with it. Buying when the market is going down is difficult.

Buying When Prices Go Down

In an annual report, Warren Buffett discussed buying when prices are down: "A short quiz: If you plan to eat hamburgers throughout your life and are not a cattle producer, should you wish for higher or lower prices for beef? Likewise, if you are going to buy a car from time to time but are not an auto manufacturer, should you prefer higher or lower car prices? These questions, of course, answer themselves."[1]

"But now," Buffett goes on, "for the final exam: If you expect to be a net saver during the next five years, should you hope for a higher or lower stock market during that period? Many investors get this one wrong. Even though they are going to be net buyers of stocks for many years to come, they are elated when stock prices rise and depressed when they fall. In effect, they rejoice because prices have risen for the 'hamburgers' they will soon be buying. This reaction makes no sense. Only those who will be sellers of equities in the near future should be happy at seeing stocks rise. Prospective purchasers should much prefer sinking prices."

What he is getting at is that we should be happy to buy when prices are low. But the difficulty is that everyone else is selling, the market is falling, and the newspapers are predicting worse to come. People who can invest when the market is falling are rare. Dollar cost averaging solves this problem by buying every month whether the market is up or down.

The Great Crash of 1929

Note the averages at the bottom of the table. We calculated the averages with and without the Great Crash of 1929. Is it reasonable to exclude the Great Depression from our analysis?

I believe that a market crash like the crash of 1929, which wiped out 89% of the value of the market, is quite unlikely to happen in the present environment. For one thing, the margin requirements were only 10% which means investors could be wiped out if the market dropped more than 10%, and many investors were using margin.

Here is a quote from an interview with Walter Morgan who founded the Wellington Mutual Fund in 1928. How would you like to start a mutual fund one year before the crash of 1929?

"How would you describe the stock market in the late 1920s?"

"Business was good, earnings were high, and stocks were selling at fifty and sixty times earnings. Investors were highly leveraged, and everybody thought they could make a fortune in the market. There was so much speculation, and stocks were just too high. Bonds and preferreds, on the other hand, were selling at a considerable discount—40 to 50 cents on the dollar."

"Do you see any parallels with today's stock market environment?"

"There was more speculation back then. You could borrow money very easily to buy stocks, and nearly everybody was highly leveraged. For instance, you could buy $10,000 worth of stocks and put up only $1,000 or so. When things turned the other way, egad, people lost their shirts."[2]

Mr. Morgan is referring to investing using borrowed money, margin investing. What happened is that before banks and brokers could "buy in" the margin investor's equity, the market had dropped below the point where the loan was recoverable. This left the banks with bad loans. Then the problem spread to real estate because investors began selling their real estate to pay off their bad margin loans. With real estate prices falling, these investors went bankrupt and the banks had more bad loans.

For example, a bank loans $90,000 to a margin investor who puts up $10,000 and buys $100,000 of stock. Then the stock falls suddenly to $70,000, and the investor's equity is erased; the bank can only recover $70,000 of the $90,000 loan. Since the investor still owes $20,000 to the bank, he tries to sell his house to pay the debt. If he had a $100,000 house with an $80,000 mortgage that might be possible. But since everyone is trying to sell real estate at the same time, the price of his house falls to $60,000. Now the investor is bankrupt and two banks have bad loans.

Then the banks began to fail, and with the bank failures, people's savings accounts were wiped out. So everyone stopped buying goods and services, and more people lost their jobs because everyone ran out of money. The market dropped from 381 in November 1929 to 41 in July 1932, a decline of 89%. Unemployment reached 33%.

Because of that disaster, today margin rules are 50% equity for initial margin and 35% equity for maintenance margin. That means investors must own 35% of any margin position; thus, the market must drop suddenly more than 35% before there can be any loss to the lender. If the borrower's equity drops to 35%, the bank sells the stock and pays off the loan and gives any change to the investor. The federal government insures banks up to $100,000 per depositor. We are not operating in the same economic climate, and I believe that you do not have to plan to survive a great crash.

Surviving Market Declines

But there were still four declines since 1914 that exceeded 40%, excluding the Great Depression. You should expect to weather such a decline if you are going to be invested for life. The decline from January 1973 to December 1974 lasted twenty-three months and took the market down 45%.

How are we going to get through the ups and downs of the market? In the previous chapter you saw that long-term holding periods minimized the risk of down markets. But even though long-term investors win in the end, we still have to survive the voyage. In addition to investing for the long term, we should use an entry strategy to avoid buying at a market high. Dollar cost averaging is one strategy; buying when the market is falling is another strategy.

Second, we need to expect that we will have to weather a market decline sometime and not get stuck needing the money when the market is down. Remember suitability? If we only invest long-term money in the stock market, we will never need to sell during a decline. We can use declines as buying opportunities. But how long is a decline? Look at our data above: between two weeks and five years, the average being fifteen months.

How Long Is a Dip?

How long does it takes the market to go down is only half the question. How long does it then take to go back up? The right side of the table shows when the Dow Jones Industrial Average recovered the high price it had achieved before the decline began. In personal terms, this answers the question, "If I bought at the high price and the market then went down, how long did it take for the market to recover to the level at which I invested?"

The worst row in our table is the Great Depression. From the high of September 3, 1929, the market declined until July 8, 1932, or three years. And the market did not recover to the 1929 high level until November 23, 1954, twenty-five years later. But, if we can exclude the Great Depression from our consideration, then the longest full down market cycle lasted from January 1973 until November 1982, almost ten years.

Note that the average time to decline was fifteen months, the average time to recover was thirty months, and the average total months was forty-six, or about four years. If we remove the Great Depression, then these averages become fourteen months to decline, eighteen months to recover and thirty-three months total, or about an average of three years from buying at the top until you are back at the same price level.

These are long times to wait. Can we avoid buying at the top? Out of the 21,000 days between 1914 and 2000, these high dates are the twenty-one worst days to buy. There are 999 chances out of 1,000 that you would not buy at the high before a major decline. We wanted to see how bad it could get, and this is the worst. So let's make a statement: "If you invested on one of the twenty-one worst possible days in the past eighty-six years, you would, on average, have waited three or four years until the market recovered to the high at which you invested."

History Plus Insight

What conclusion can we draw from looking at this history of market declines? One interesting conclusion is that the maximum declines (with the exception of the Great Depression) were 45% to 50%, which means cutting your portfolio in half. But if your money has doubled since you invested, then your original investment is protected. You occupy a secure position because it would take a market decline greater than all the declines of the twentieth century (excepting the Great Depression) to threaten your principle. And we have seen the market doubling a portfolio of index funds on average every five to six years.

Another conclusion is that there are two sides to every coin. While we have plotted significant market declines and calculated the number of months to recover, we have also plotted the twenty-one best buying opportunities of the twentieth century.

Buying When Prices Are Low

Let's suppose that the market is down –20%, and you are thinking about investing because prices are low. But you are worried that the market might continue to fall to –40%. One conclusion you could draw is that even if the market did fall to –40%, a decline to –40% is only a 25% decline to someone who invested when it was at –20%. For example, if the market is at 100 and will decline to 60 (–40%), to someone who invests at 80 the decline to 60 is a 25% decline. Therefore, buying when the market is already down reduces your risk of a decline. Another conclusion is that since the market has recovered from every decline in the past, it will also recover from future declines. Therefore, if your investment horizon is long term, you expect to recover from the current decline. In addition, if you invest when the market is down –20%, then your time to recover will arrive faster since you are aiming for a target that is –20% lower than the previous high. And when the market reaches it's previous high, you will be in the black by 25%. In short, if you invest when the market is down, it reduces the risk of decline, it speeds the time of recovery, and it increases future returns.

On the other hand, if you sell when the market goes down, you sell at the low, you incur the capital gains tax, you miss the rally that follows the decline, and you miss an opportunity to buy more when prices are down.

What Does This Mean to You?

This means that you should understand the risks of investing. You must study carefully the table of the biggest market drops. You must tell yourself before the market falls that you will ride it out, that you will stay in for the long term. If the front page of the newspaper declares "The stock market is falling!", you will laugh, knowing that this is a chance for a long-term investor like yourself to buy when prices are low.

But this kind of bravado in the face of mass hysteria does not come easily. We can predict that if the market declines for fourteen months, and loses 25% of its value (an average decline), many people will panic and sell their investments. If the S&P 500 were to decline 25%, then some popular stocks would decline 80%. In addition, the news media will write stories about investors who are making big money selling stocks short. Someone will predict that the decline could become "worse," and that prediction will get a lot of media attention. These ideas will affect your judgment, and you will wonder if you did the "right thing" putting all your money into stocks. You may engage in some "nail biting" before the decline is over and the market begins to recover. Whatever you do will be fine as long as you do not sell when prices are down, because you are certain to reduce your long-term return if you sell under pressure when the market is down.

When it is time to sell there must be a reason and a purpose. You need the money to repay a debt, to pay for a house, to retire, for college, or you wish to give money to charity. Selling because you fear for the future is not a sufficient reason. But if you have followed the suitability guidelines, then you have invested only long-term money in stocks, and there is no good reason to sell when the market is down.

Now the Good News

But you said that the S&P 500 Index has earned 14⅞% over the past twenty years? How can that be, since three of the top twenty-one declines have occurred in the past twenty years? The answer is that even though the market goes down, it goes up more often. The return has been great on average. But while we invest for the long term, we read the newspaper daily. We need to refocus on our long-term investment horizon. We need to remind ourselves that the index represents the leading 500 companies in the U.S., their sales around the world, their employees, and their innovations. I have no doubt that as long as we live, this country and the workers in the 500 leading companies will continue to exist and prosper. There is no surer investment than the top companies in the United States. There is no return that is more certain to outperform other investments.

The flip side of bear markets is bull markets. For every decline, there has been a subsequent market rise. The market has gone up more than down, and market advances have been longer than declines. Therefore, the probability of investing when prices are rising is better than fifty-fifty. Therefore, if it is an average day, it is good for investing.

Stock Market Rises

Where are the profits? How do people make money in the stock market? Here are the market advances above 25%. Coincidentally, there are also twenty-one events, the same as the number of market declines below 20%. Please note that it takes a 25% up move to recover from a 20% down move. If you have $100 and lose 20% you end up with $80. To get from $80 back to $100 requires a 25% up move.

Buy Date	Sell Date	Max. Advance	Avg. Advance	Up Months
6/9/15	11/21/16	64%	42%	17.4
5/26/15	11/3/19	86%	50%	53.0
22/24/15	9/3/29	603%	232%	174.3
11/13/29	4/17/30	48%	32%	5.1
6/2/31	7/3/31	128%	28%	1.0
10/5/31	11/9/31	135%	35%	1.1
7/27/32	9/7/32	56%	41%	1.3
5/26/33	7/18/33	26%	26%	1.7
10/20/33	2/5/34	28%	27%	3.5
10/30/34	3/10/37	109%	62%	28.3
3/31/38	11/9/38	60%	42%	7.3
4/11/39	9/12/39	26%	26%	5.0
8/8/45	5/29/46	31%	29%	9.7
10/28/58	12/13/61	37%	31%	37.5
11/20/62	2/9/66	57%	40%	38.6
10/7/66	12/3/68	32%	29%	25.9
10/29/62	1/11/73	82%	50%	122.4
4/7/75	9/21/76	37%	32%	17.5
4/23/80	4/27/81	130%	28%	12.1
9/29/86	8/25/87	55%	41%	10.9
5/9/89	9/16/90	27%	26%	14.2
Averages		74.1%	45.2%	28.0

The average bull market advance lifts the Dow Jones Industrial Average 74% and lasts twenty-eight months. Comparing just the major advances to declines, we see the average up market was

45%, the average decline, 26%. If we start with $100 and lose 26%, we will have $74. Then, if the market goes up 45%, we will earn $33.40 and finish with $107.40. Therefore, in considering only the twenty-one largest declines and the twenty-one largest advances, we see an overall positive trend. The count was the same for both, indicating that there is an equal opportunity to buy at the bottom of a future up market or to buy at the top of a future down market.

Positive Trend in Stock Prices Since 1914

What should you be getting from this? A feel for the worst weather that your Personal Endowment Account could be getting into. An understanding of how the market will treat you. Patience that looks beyond the daily ups and downs and says, "We win in the end if we can ride it out." The sober realization that you might fail to ride it out; therefore, you better know what your goals are before you get in.

The excess average return of the major up markets over the major down markets was only 7.4%. Why so low? The Dow Jones Industrial Average is a price index. The values that were used for this analysis did not include dividends. Therefore, these are prices only, not total returns. If you were to buy an index fund, you would reinvest your dividends and increase your return.

Like Cutting Down a Tree and Looking At the Rings

We all know that when a tree is chopped down there is a ring for every year. Some very old redwood trees go back over two thousand years. Scientists have discovered that a detailed inspection of the rings reveals the weather patterns in the different years. A very rainy year will produce a lot of growth and all the trees will have a correspondingly wide ring for that year. A drought will stunt the growth of trees. A skilled scientist could create a chart of the maximum and minimum and average amounts of tree growth for all of the historical data available in a particular region. When we include petrified wood and fossils, that would be thousands of years.

How does this relate to your investment portfolio? The bull and bear markets that we have been studying represent the maximum and minimum and average portfolio growth in each of the years since 1914. We cannot predict the future with absolute certainty anymore than we can predict next year's rainfall or tree growth. But we can certainly predict that trees will grow. How much will they grow? About as much as they have generally been growing in the past. We can predict that the top 500 companies in the U.S. will grow. How much will they grow? About as much as they have been growing in the past.

People get excited about hurricanes, tornadoes, droughts, blizzards, heat waves, and sunny weekends. But when you look back at the past it all blends together. The market is not very different. There are up markets, down markets, crashes, rallies, wars, recessions, and bull markets. When we look back we see that it all blends together and only a few salient points are memorable.

CHAPTER 12

How Big Are Our Profits?

NOW LET'S LOOK AT HOW MUCH MONEY WE MAKE. The annualized total return for the period June 30, 1936, to March 31, 1998, was 12.04%, and that sounds nice. But one dollar invested on June 30, 1936, grew to $1,397, and that sounds much nicer. Imagine that if

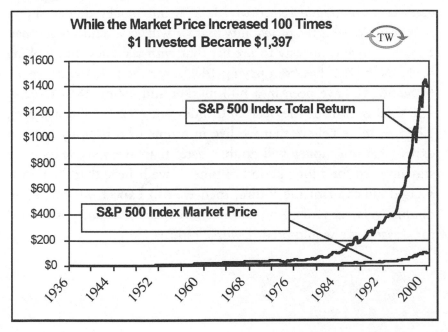

you had invested $10,000, it would be worth $10,301,300 and still growing. Do you know anywhere else where you can reasonably expect to receive $1,030 dollars for each dollar that you invest? Now we will look at how much our investments grow when invested for a long period. The graph on the previous page shows two lines, Market Prices and Total Returns. Total Returns grow dramatically the longer we stay invested.

Can You Expect Your Money to Double Every Five Years?

We have been using 14⅞% as a target rate of return on index funds. But what is the risk that you will not realize 14⅞% compound returns? The market's ups and downs will definitely change your return. What effect will that higher or lower compound rate of return have on this program?

We learn from this table that if the market gives us a compound return of 12.25%, our money doubles every six years. If the market gives us a compound return of 18.92%, our money doubles every four years. What is the probability that we will get a return other than 14⅞%? There is no way to predict that with accuracy. But looking back, the market has been paying 14⅞% for the past twenty years. Recently, we have been in a bull market and seeing 18% returns. The total return for the S&P 500 Index since 6/30/1936 has been 12.25%. If we believe that we live in a time of prosperity, we can expect that our money will double faster than every six years if we stay invested for a long period of time. If we believe that the past is a good indicator of the future, then we can expect our money to double every six years. And if we believe that the country is headed for disaster, we would predict worse returns.

Spreadsheet of Time to Double

Compound Rate of Return	Time to Double in Years	Rule of 72	Rule of 72
100.00%	1	100	This chart can be memorized using the "Rule of 72." The product of any two numbers on each row equals approximately 72 for most of the returns. Therefore, if you want to know what rate will double your money in six years, divide 72 by six and the answer is 12%. If you want to know how fast a rate of 10% will double your money, divide 72 by 10 and the answer is 7.2 years.
41.42%	2	83	
25.99%	3	78	
18.92%	4	76	
14.875%	5	74	
12.25%	6	74	
10.41%	7	73	
9.05%	8	72	
8.00%	9	72	
7.17%	10	72	
6.51%	11	72	
5.94%	12	71	
5.47%	13	71	
5.07%	14	71	
4.72%	15	71	
2.00%	35	70	

Graphs of Total Return

To check this hypothesis we drew graphs of the historical total return on the S&P 500 since 1936 using one-, five-, ten-, fifteen-, twenty-, twenty-five-, thirty-, and forty-year investment periods. The past is no guarantee of the future, but it should give us a confidence interval. History should show us whether we can believe what we have been saying and how wrong we could be and still be in reality.

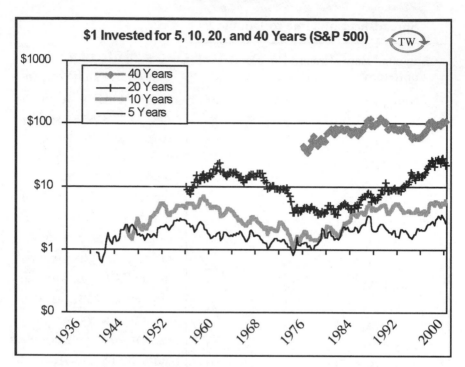

$1 Invested for 5, 10, 20, and 40 Years (S&P 500)

This chart has the return from investing one dollar for five, ten, twenty, and forty years. Each quarter we started with one dollar and five years later we recorded how much the dollar had grown. We know mathematically that one dollar will double if the growth rate is 14⅞%. By looking at the five-year line, we can see that sometimes after five years the value was below one dollar, meaning we lost money. The highest value was $3.42, and the average was $1.82. So the market has generally delivered a doubling of investors' money every five years since 1936, even when all the low spots are included. Please note that the scale of the graph is logarithmic to allow visual separation of the lines. These results are summarized in the following table:

Spreadsheet of Total Returns, 1936 to 2000

$1 invested in the S&P 500 Index became $x.xx in yy Years: from June 30, 1936, until September 29, 2000									
	1 year	5 years	10 years	15 years	20 years	25 years	30 years	40 years	60 years
average	$1.13	$1.87	$3.48	$6.49	$10.92	$16.79	$25.17	$78.60	$1,134.35
max	$1.61	$3.51	$6.87	$13.97	$28.64	$53.57	$58.76	$119.88	$1,688.62
min	$0.51	$0.60	$1.05	$1.83	$3.51	$6.03	$13.51	$33.31	$560.86

Are Things Different Now?

Looking at results since 1936 may not be relevant if the world has changed. Do you believe that the market has been more prosperous recently? Do you believe that this more prosperous world will persist into the future? Since 1980, the market has been earning higher returns than previously.

Spreadsheet of the Most Recent Total Returns

$1 invested in the S&P 500 Index became $x.xx in yy Years: using results for the most recent 10 years ending September 29, 2000									
	1 year	5 years	10 years	15 years	20 years	25 years	30 years	40 years	60 years
average	$1.18	$2.28	$3.99	$6.13	$9.33	$16.79	$25.17	$78.68	$1,134.35
max	$1.47	$3.51	$5.91	$13.97	$28.64	$53.57	$58.76	$119.88	$1,688.62
min	$0.91	$1.52	$1.63	$2.16	$3.51	$6.03	$13.51	$33.31	$560.86

If we look at this table showing the results for the most recent ten years, we see the five-year average result was $1.00 becomes $2.04. To calculate the five-year average from quarter to quarter, we had to start fifteen years back to March 1983. The ten-year average result was $1.00 becomes $4.37, twice doubling. Of course, those calculations began in March 1978. The fifteen-year average was $1.00 becomes $8.37, three times doubling, and those calculations began in March 1973. The twenty-year total return shows $1.00 becoming $11.72, not a fourth doubling. Why? The twenty-year calculations began in March 1968, and the market did not rise from 1969 to 1979. This decade of poor returns coincided with the Vietnam War and accompanying inflation and affects the twenty, twenty-five, and thirty-year results. But see how the forty-year results are much higher at an average of $84. The forty-year results began in March 1948, and the market rose through the 1950s.

The conclusion, then, is that the market has clearly been doubling consistently every five years for the past fifteen years. But a future war or inflation could put the brakes on the market. Also, a look at the minimum returns should remind you that having to take your money out when the market is down could cost you the good returns that you hoped to achieve. We conclude that this shows that the returns we have been speaking about, 14⅞% and doubling every five years, are actual and probably repeatable. But we should leave ourselves a big margin for lower returns by only investing money in our PEA for life and expecting conservative growth. If our money stays in the market for life, then it can ride through the periods of poor returns.

When We Speak of Your Money Doubling

In this book we frequently refer to money doubling every five years. We are assuming a long-term investment horizon when we say this. When we spoke of owning a car for five years while your PEA doubles, we did not mean that you could be sure to double your money in a specific five-year period. (If you only invest for five years, you should expect that each dollar could become 60 cents or $3.42, or anything in between.) But if you are invested for life, then you can say that while you owned a car for five years, your PEA doubled because on average your PEA doubled every five years.

Also, please understand that money has been doubling every five years only for the past fifteen years. Since 1936, returns have been lower; money has been doubling every six years. Therefore, when we say that your money doubles every five years, we are assuming a continuation of relatively recent results. To be conservative, you should expect lower returns, such as doubling every six years. Then you can be happy if the market does better than you expected.

CHAPTER 13

Alternative Investments

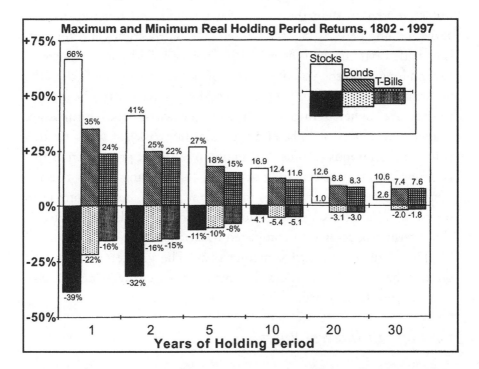

Maximum and Minimum Real Holding Period Returns, 1802 - 1997

Stocks
Bonds
T-Bills

	1	2	5	10	20	30
Stocks	66%	41%	27%	16.9	12.6	10.6
Bonds	35%	25%	18%	12.4	8.8	7.4
T-Bills	24%	22%	15%	11.6	8.3	7.6

1.0
2.6

-4.1 -5.4 -5.1
-3.1 -3.0
-2.0 -1.8

-11% -10% -8%

-16%
-22%

-16% -15%

-39%
-32%

Years of Holding Period

COULD YOU DO BETTER INVESTING YOUR MONEY ELSEWHERE? This chart from Jeremy Siegel's book *Stocks for the Long Run* shows both the consistency of long-term returns and the return advantage of stocks over bonds and bills. The time period, 1802 to 1997, includes every market move in the history of the United States, and we can see that given a twenty-year holding period, stocks never lost money. The same cannot be said for bonds and bills.

If you notice that these returns are lower than the 14⅞% that we have been using, it is because these are the average returns since 1802 adjusted for inflation. In addition, we need mentally to reduce the returns on bonds and bills by the taxes we would have to pay each year.

Also, note that the higher volatility of the stock market disappears with holding periods of ten, twenty, or thirty years. You can see this in the graph. The white/black bar (stock returns) is much taller (vertically) than the shaded bars (bond and bill returns) for short holding periods, but the white/black bar becomes shorter than the shaded bars in the longer holding periods. Did you expect this? Over a long term the volatility (risk) of stock returns is less than the volatility of bonds or bill returns. For longer terms, the best stock returns are higher than bonds or bills, the worst stock returns are higher than bonds or bills, and the volatility (risk) of stock returns is lower than bonds or bills. For many investment professionals this is a revelation. It is generally accepted that buying bonds reduces your risk. For short-term investments that is true, but for long-term investment horizons this has not been true. Bonds only provide short-term risk reduction compared to stocks.

Have you ever heard someone say, "The greater the risk, the greater the reward"? This graph is proof that we can reduce the risk and increase the reward.

Changes in Interest Rates

The next chart is the interest rate on corporate bonds rated BAA since January 1947. (The bond rating BAA is the highest yielding investment grade corporate bond rating. That means your investment is considered secure.) The average bond interest rate has been about 6%. But the after-tax returns are even worse than that because individuals pay tax each year on interest income; therefore, a 6% bond to a person who pays taxes of 40% gives an after-tax return of 3.6%. Going back to our table of the number of years to double, we see that at 3.6% it takes more than fifteen years to double.

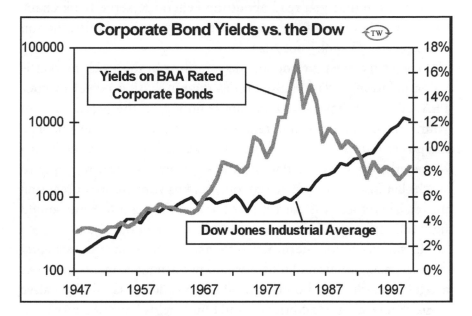

Note that the peak in interest rates was 17.18% in February 1982. And 17.18% after taxes of 40% is 10.40%; therefore, even the peak interest rates did not beat the average long-term stock returns for a taxable investor.

Now consider the other line on this chart, the Dow Jones Industrial Average. Note on the logarithmic scale that the market climbed from 100+ in 1947 to about 1,000 in 1966, then was basically flat, around 1,000, from 1966 to 1982, and then began to climb again from 1982 until 2000. The rate of climb has been about the same in the past eighteen years as it was from 1947 to 1966. The flat spot in the stock market coincides with the climb in interest rates from 5% in 1966 to 17% in 1982. When interest rates began to go back down, the market began to rise. The cause of the high interest rates between 1966 and 1982 was the inflation that was introduced to finance the national debt. Only when the U.S. government stopped inflating the currency and Fed chairman Paul Volcker forced interest rates higher did inflation begin to abate. So the next time that you read about the Federal Reserve Bank chairman, Alan Greenspan, managing interest rates to check inflation you can say, "Thank you, Alan."

The prime enemy to double digit returns in the stock market is rising inflation. Inflation also erodes the purchasing power of your PEA. After you have saved and are counting on the proceeds from your PEA to support you in retirement, you could see your purchasing power reduced if inflation should rise. So, while everyone likes a bull market in stocks, inflation causes greater damage, not only to stocks but also to the whole economy and to your future purchasing power. Therefore, it is correct that the Federal Reserve Bank should fight inflation, even if it causes stocks to fall temporarily.

In summary, long-term investments in stocks have consistently outperformed bonds and bills. Also, long-term investments in stocks are less volatile than bonds and bills. Considered as an alternative to stock investing, even brief rises in bond yields have not surpassed the long-term returns for an index investor when viewed on an after-tax basis. Therefore, for an index investor with a long-term horizon, there is no incentive to invest in bonds or bills in order to increase total return.

Chapter 14
Total Benefits

In summary of Part 1, "The Big Idea": A passive index fund investor can outperform almost all active portfolio managers on an after-tax basis if he or she invests for the long term. And he will do this with more certainty and less effort. Furthermore, he can improve these certain returns by dollar cost averaging. In addition, using the endowment lifestyle, he can expect to have more money compounding tax deferred for a longer time. When he adds up all these benefits, how much has he improved his total wealth?

Benefits from Index Fund Investing

From Chapter 3, we learned that the savings from investing in index funds were:

Index funds over average equity managers	+2%
Savings in expenses and taxes	+4.5%
Total Savings	+6.5%

Look at the Time to Double Spreadsheet. When we consider the long-term return on the market, we cannot add 6½% because we are efficient. Instead, we avoid 6½% in inefficiencies. Therefore, if after taxes and fees your index funds earn 14%, the average investor suffering from typical inefficiencies would keep 6½% less, or 6½%. Using the table of Time to Double in Years, we see that 14% versus 7% is the difference between doubling every five years or doubling every ten years. And the lower the overall level of returns, the greater the effect of a 6½% improvement. For instance, if index funds earn 12%, then the average investor would keep 5½%. If the index funds earn 10%, then the average investor would keep 3½%.

Time to Double Spreadsheet

Time to Double in Years	Compound Rate of Return
3	25.99%
4	18.92%
5	14.87%
6	12.25%
7	10.41%
8	9.05%
9	8.00%
10	7.17%
11	6.51%
12	5.94%

Total Return from the Endowment Lifestyle

On top of the benefits of long-term index investing, we are suggesting an endowment lifestyle where the investor leaves his or her endowment compounding at equity market rates of return and uses less expensive borrowed money to purchase items of value, such as houses and cars. It is difficult to express just how much the endowment lifestyle will increase the size of your PEA, because the benefits grow over time. The longer you allow your PEA to compound undisturbed the larger it becomes. If we compare a save and spend lifestyle to an endowment lifestyle, the endowment balance will be larger, but how much larger depends on how many times the individual held onto the money that he or she would have spent in the past.

For theoretical purposes, let's suppose that an individual manages to keep twice as much money invested by using these principles. The first half of the money earns the index fund rate, and the second half of the money earns the index fund rate minus borrowing costs. Let's say that equals 4%. Thus, we could say that the contribution of the endowment lifestyle is 2% to the whole portfolio.

This return improvement from practicing the endowment lifestyle can be added to our market return. Therefore, if we receive 14% from the market, we can add our 2% endowment lifestyle return, giving us an effective 16% annual return on the total wealth that passes through our hands. This is a 8½% annual return advantage over the 7½% return of the average market participant. But how can we compare earning 7½% on our small savings to earning 16% on all the money that flows through our hands during our life? We have been accustomed to saving and then spending to buy a car. Then we save and spend again to buy a house. Then we save and spend again to pay for college. Then we save and spend again to live in retirement. Suppose we don't tear down our endowment each time? How large would it get?

Wow!

All I can say is, Wow! Rearranging our lifestyle has more than doubled our rate of return. We have moved from uncertain investments yielding low returns, to certain investments yielding high returns. And these higher returns are being earned on a much larger endowment!

And the change to our life is not a big change. We still hold the same job, we still have the same living expenses, and we still save the same amount. But our total wealth is growing faster than before.

It's what we don't do that is changing our life. We don't study the market. We don't trade actively. We don't invest on stock tips and hunches. We don't subscribe to investment magazines. We don't have complicated tax returns. We don't pay cash for major expenses. And having eliminated all these time-consuming activities, our total return has increased, our endowment has increased, our free time has increased, and our worry has decreased.

Symbiotic Relationship

Lots of people own index funds. And endowments have been around for centuries. Index funds and endowments are valid by themselves, but the combination of the two gives us the extraordinary benefits. Besides increasing our total return, the endowment lifestyle increases our account balance and our holding period. This allows compounding to work its magic, deferred taxes and reduced expenses begin to make a significant contribution, and the risk of loss is greatly reduced. Index funds provide stability and certainty, which allows us to invest our total net worth in one place. Without total commitment, the endowment lifestyle cannot produce such dramatic results.

Total Commitment

One of the nice things about finding a good thing is that you can commit totally to it. The historical certainty of stock market growth, combined with market averages and dollar cost averaging and long-term investing, produces a solid, reliable, and predictable plan.

Once we know that it is going to work, we are comfortable with a total commitment. And total commitment has its own advantage.

Why? Even we can get one thing right! And when the best returns come from one simple thing, then we can earn the best returns on our total portfolio. Since we are suggesting leveraging our cars and house and college expenses, we have now committed not only our portfolio but also our total wealth.

Are you interested in learning more? Read on.

PART 2:
PUTTING YOUR PLAN
INTO ACTION

CHAPTER 15
Entering the Market

HOW DO WE AVOID BUYING AT THE TOP and selling at the bottom? If you were looking closely at the return charts in Chapter 10, "Minimizing Stock Market Risk," you would have seen a decline in 1936. People who invested $1.00 saw it go to $0.65 by 1937. This 35% decline could have been reduced by employing a market entrance strategy designed to avoid buying at a high point before a decline. If you refer back to the chart of the declines in the Dow since 1914, the average decline was always smaller than the maximum decline (obviously). Total return is based on the purchase price and the sale price, plus reinvested dividends. Therefore, we look at market entry and market exit to increase our total return. We want to avoid buying at tops and selling at bottoms. Rule number one is that dollar cost averaging will reduce your risk of investing all your money at the top.

If you recall, dollar cost averaging is investing equal amounts at regular intervals. When the market is up, you buy less stock for your money, but when the market is down, you buy more stock for the same amount of money. This keeps you from investing all your money at a single high price, and it weights your purchases more towards the lower prices. Therefore, you win in two ways.

Market Timing

By now you may have realized that we do not believe people can time market exits and entries to achieve superior returns. If people could do that, then some clever market timer would start a mutual fund called the Market Timer Fund and beat the market, and we could all give him, or her, our money to invest. Since people have been trying to do that since the stock market began, and since no one is consistently doing it, let's all take a deep breath and agree that it can't be done, and we will resist the temptation to try.

Should we risk being redundant to drive this point in? Every active money manager is trying to beat the market. Mark Twain said, "It is easy to beat the market, just buy at the bottom and sell at the top." Since the people with billions to invest and millions to spend to help them analyze everything from the economy to the stars have not been able to beat the market averages consistently, we conclude that it is neither easy nor probable. But human nature being what it is, we are all tempted to try to time market exits and entrances. Therefore, resist the temptation to invest impulsively and stick with a plan.

Here is some quantitative evidence. Using the total return data on the S&P 500 Index since June 30, 1936, we have 258 quarters whose average quarterly return is 12.52%. By sorting them in descending order and removing the top twenty-five quarters (10%), the average return drops to 7.02%. That means that 10% of the time is when the market earns its superior returns, and if you are not in the market and fully invested, you could miss the periods when the market goes up. Then we calculated the same average removing only the six best quarters, and the average dropped from 12.52% to 10.97%. Even removing the top 2% of the periods hurts our average return. The point is that it is very difficult to be right all the time, and if you miss just a few up markets, it will significantly reduce the total return.

To drub the point once again, we counted the number of up days and down days in each year. There are just as many up days and down days whether it was an up market or a down market. In up markets the up days were a little better on average than the down days, and vice versa. But the market changes direction just as often when it goes up as when it goes down. Can you reasonably expect to be in the market on up days and out on down days? Can you expect to be in the market on up months and out on down months or in on up years and out on down years? If you are beginning to feel that you can't time the market, you're in good company because no one else can either. Therefore, let's stop chasing rainbows and get back to work.

When You Enter the Market

What situations might you find yourself in regarding market entry?

Actively Managed Portfolio

You may have a portfolio of stocks now and decide that you want to buy index funds. We will call this an actively managed portfolio. In that case you are already in the market, and therefore the main decision is capital gains taxes. The stocks that have no significant capital gains tax exposure can be sold, and you can buy index funds in a lump. More about minimizing capital gains in the next chapter.

If a particular stock in your actively managed portfolio is beaten down, and you believe that it should recover, then you should wait and see if it will go up relative to the market. On the other hand, if the market is down and all your stocks are down, it makes no difference when you switch to an index fund for it will be down also. In fact, switching when prices are low will reduce your capital gains taxes.

Lump Sum Investment

Perhaps you have inherited some money or sold a house. We will call this a lump sum. After you decide what your time horizon is, and after you have made the allocation decision (Chapter 5), you have a lump sum to invest. Put it into a money market fund and each month for twelve months invest one-twelfth in the chosen index fund. Or you could divide it into three pieces. Or you could invest each quarter. Most mutual funds groups have automatic investment plans, and they will automatically invest on a periodic basis for you. The point is that you should review the tables in the chapter on risk and decide what kind of dollar cost averaging is agreeable to you and to your acceptable level of risk. Then find a fund and tell the mutual funds people to make the periodic investments for you, lest you forget.

Regular Investing

Perhaps you have an income and you want to invest a sum regularly. Then set up an automatic withdrawal program with your checking or savings account. Each month the money will be automatically invested.

Perhaps you get a bonus once a year, and you want to invest a portion of it regularly. You could put the bonus in a money market account and have it invested regularly during the year.

Less Than a Lump Sum

You may have a sum of money, which is less than a lump sum. Just put it in the market as soon as you can. "He that observes the wind shall not sow, and he that regards the clouds shall not reap" (Ecclesiastes 11:4). The meaning of this proverb is that if you spend too much time looking at the Weather Channel, you won't plant your seeds or reap your harvest. Therefore, don't over worry, just choose your plan and then do it. It may help if you reassure yourself that the goal is to get an average return. Therefore, if it is an average day, it is perfect for investing.

Market Timing for Long-term Index Investors

Having scared you away from timing the market, I have to confess that in a limited fashion it is possible to improve your chances. Let's assume that you have bought into this dollar cost averaging plan and each month you invest your regular amount. When the market is rising, it is important to keep investing for it may never come back down. The low price that is available today may never be available again. Therefore, any delay in investing will cost you.

But sometimes the market experiences a major shock. You read in the paper that the Dow is down 15% or 20%, and coupled with this news some people are predicting that it could get worse before it gets better. You immediately pull this book off your shelf and go to the table on market declines since 1914 and note with amazement that the present market move has made the chart! This is, in fact, a "big decline." What should you do?

The reason that we dollar cost average is to avoid investing all our money at a market high. The second reason is to accumulate more shares when prices are low. If you know that the market is 15% below a high, then you have satisfied both goals. Therefore, buy more than your usual periodic amount. If you plan to invest three times in the next three months, then you could accelerate that and invest it all today while the market is down.

You will naturally ask, "What if the market continues to go down?" First, is that a valid concern? Aren't you happy to buy 15% below a market high? Last month you invested at the list price, and you would have been very happy to buy at 15% off.

Second, you could divide your money into two parts, invest half now, and invest again if the market goes farther down. At least you will be putting some extra money into the market when it is down.

What differentiates this strategy from market timing, which we do not believe we can succeed at? Here we are committed to investing regularly, every month, for some future period of months. We are willing to accept whatever purchase price the market offers on the day we have chosen to invest. We expect that we will achieve a purchase cost that is not at the high, but at the average. Now, if the market falls to a level that our historical tables tell us is below average, then we can confidently put our money into the market knowing that we are buying at below the average cost. The questions "How far below average?" and "Will it go lower tomorrow?" become less relevant. If you can buy when stocks are "on sale," do it and stop worrying. If you hesitate the price may go up again.

Another difference between market timing and buying when prices are down is that market timing requires correctly executing three trades to our one trade. First, the market timer must buy low; second, the market timer must sell higher; third, the market timer must buy something else. But we buy and hold for life. Therefore, we only have to execute one trade correctly. If we know that the index is down, then we buy more.

A truly significant question is, "Where do I find the money?" This is difficult because if you are investing your money, it is already in the market. Most people can only obtain additional funds by looking a few months forward. Therefore, as good as this entry strategy sounds, it probably will not increase your returns significantly.

Also, this fortuitous event cannot be anticipated. Suppose that you had a lump sum to invest in the coming year and you decided that you would wait until the market went down to invest it all. With your luck, the market would probably go up or flat, but not down, for the next few years. Then on December 31 you would have to make your investment in one lump at the highest price of the year. Therefore, we'll just have to stick to our boring plan. There is very little excitement in making money.

Summary: Entering the Market

To boil this down to a simple investing plan do the following. Decide how much money you will be able to put into your PEA in the coming year. Set up an automatic investment plan that will invest for you each month or quarter. With this automatic plan, you will participate if the market is rising. Then if the market drops to a low level, you can consider buying more than your regular monthly amount. Thus, you will buy well in a rising market and in a falling market.

Chapter 16

Tax Strategies

In this chapter, we will look at some suggestions on how to avoid, defer, or reduce taxes to the minimum.

Capital Gains Taxes

We keep mentioning capital gains taxes. At the moment the federal tax rate is 20% on gains from investments held over twelve months. Gains on investments held less than twelve months are taxed at your ordinary income tax rate. This means that if you buy a fund for $100, it doubles to $200, and you sell it after twelve months, you owe a 20% tax on the gain of $100, or $20. If you sell it before twelve months you have a short-term gain which is taxed at your ordinary income tax rate. Most states and some municipalities also charge taxes on long- and short-term gains, so your actual tax is higher.

The first thing to know about capital gains taxes is that they change frequently. What can you do about Washington changing the rules? Not much. Be happy: if you wait long enough, you might not have to pay. That's right; at the moment there are no capital gains taxes on inheritances. When you die, your heirs receive your investments at the current market value, and your cost basis is forgotten. That's one way to avoid the capital gains tax.

Sale by Lot

Another way to minimize capital gains taxes is to keep records of all your purchases and sales and capital gains distributions and reinvested dividends. Then you are able to sell by lot. To sell by lot you must specify to the broker or mutual fund that you are selling a lot purchased on a specific date and give the date. They will then print that on the confirmation. For example: You bought one hundred shares of a mutual fund each year for five years, at prices of $100, $110, $120, $130, and then $140 on 12/31/95. Now the price is $200, and you wish to sell one hundred shares. If you do not specify a sale by lot, then you must use the average purchase price of $120 to calculate the capital gain tax. If you wish to use the purchase at $140 to minimize your capital gain, you must specify at the time of the sale, "Sale versus Lot of 12/31/95." This also means that you should do your first sale by lot, because if you did the first sale using average cost, how could you later switch to the "sale by lot" method? Therefore, you can pay yourself benefits by keeping detailed records and selling by lot to minimize the capital gains tax. Many brokers and mutual fund companies automatically track your average cost basis. But you generally have to compute the sale by lot on your own.

Offset Capital Losses

Another way to avoid capital gains taxes is to lose money long term. That is because long-term losses offset long-term gains. No one likes to lose money, but when you realize a long-term loss in another security, you could sell an amount of your index fund that will create an equal gain. Then, repurchase the index fund. In effect you will remain invested, but you raise the cost basis of your index fund.

Giving to Charity

If you regularly give money to charity, you can avoid capital gains taxes by giving appreciated securities to charity. The charitable deduction you receive is equal to the market value of what you give, and capital gains taxes are not due. You may then repurchase the index fund with the cash that you would have given away. Now you have the same amount invested, but the cost basis is the market value. For example, if you invest $1,000 and ten years later it is worth $4,000, you could give the security to charity. You would receive a charitable deduction for a gift of $4,000, and no capital gains tax would be due. You could then purchase $4,000 of the same security that you gave away. Now your cost basis is $4,000, and you still own the security.

We should all be giving money to charity. And you can eliminate paying capital gains taxes via this strategy. Also, giving will increase your return. The Bible says that God blesses a cheerful giver. Jesus said that we would receive a hundred-fold return in this life (Mark 10:20). We are talking about 14⅞% returns here. Imagine if one dollar became $100. That will definitely increase your total wealth. But you have to give your money away to participate in God's investment plan. If you think investing in stocks takes faith, try investing in the kingdom of God! But remember, His benefits are eternal.

Charitable Gift Mutual Funds

A recent innovation in charitable giving is the charitable gift mutual fund. The investor donates cash or securities to the charitable fund and receives a tax deduction immediately. The fund then invests the donation until the donor instructs the fund to pay the proceeds to a charity.

One benefit is that a large gift of securities can be donated to the charitable gift fund, and then the proceeds can be distributed to several charities in smaller amounts.

A second benefit is that many small charitable organizations are not experienced in accepting gifts of securities. The charitable gift fund sells the securities without error, provides the investor accurate record keeping, and gives the money to the charity.

A third benefit is that large gifts can be made anonymously.

Here are three well-known charitable gift funds:

Schwab Fund for Charitable Giving
101 Montgomery Street
San Francisco, California 94101-9700
Phone 800-746-6216
www.schwabcharitable.org
Minimum contribution $10,000

Charitable Gift Fund, Fidelity Investments
82 Devonshire Street F1A
Boston, Massachusetts 02109-9745
Phone 800-682-4438
www.charitable-gift.org
Minimum contribution $10,000

Vanguard Charitable Endowment
PO Box 3075
Southeastern, Pennsylvania 19398-9917
Phone 888-383-4483
www.vangaurdcharitable.org
Minimum contribution $25,000

Combine Giving and Offsetting Losses

You can combine selling by lot, long-term losses, and charitable giving to optimize your tax deductions. Let's say that you bought one hundred shares at $50 and two hundred shares at $75, and now the market is at $100. Therefore, your portfolio is worth $30,000. By giving the one hundred share lot that you bought at $50 to charity you can shelter a $5,000 gain. Also, to get this $5,000 gain, you only give away $10,000. To shelter a $5,000 gain from the shares that you bought at $75, you would have to give away $20,000. So, in charitable giving, low-cost lots are better.

But if you have a $5,000 long-term capital loss from another investment, you could sell $20,000 (two hundred shares) of the index fund versus the lot you bought at $75, create a $5,000 long-term gain, and then repurchase the index fund with the proceeds of your sale. It doesn't matter which lot you use when you are offsetting a long-term loss. Therefore, when offsetting losses, high priced lots are better.

To summarize, when giving to charity, you can benefit more from low-priced lots, but when offsetting a long-term capital loss, any lot will do the job. So, save all the low priced lots for charity and always use the high-priced lots when offsetting long-term losses.

Charitable Annuity

You can also avoid capital gains taxes when it is time to exit the market by giving away the principle of your investments to charity. The charity then purchases an annuity, which pays you and your spouse an income for the rest of your life. In this way you get the full value of your investments without paying capital gains tax. The income is similar to buying a bond. You also get a charitable donation credit on your income taxes. This eliminates the inheritance for your heirs, but it takes care of you for life. The charitable annuity is a nice way to give to charity while you are alive.

Borrowing Against Your Personal Endowment Account

You can also borrow against your Personal Endowment Account to cover short-term needs without selling your securities. This avoids paying capital gains taxes. The loan will grow at the current interest rate, but your PEA will grow at the long-term market rate. Theoretically, you never need to repay the loan. The size of the loan will grow slower than your PEA. When you die the loan will be paid from the securities, and the remainder will be passed to your heirs free of capital gains taxes. More about this in Chapter 27, "Margin Accounts."

Inheritance Taxes

This is not a book about inheritance taxes. But if you follow this plan you may have substantial net worth by the time you expire. So please consult inheritance tax specialists because there are plans to avoid inheritance taxes that will benefit your heirs.

Deferring Taxes

Another thing about taxes is that the longer we defer paying the tax, the more we profit. So time is on our side. Every year that we defer the tax, we benefit. The present value of $2.00 in ten years is $1.00, at a discount rate of 8%. Therefore, any tax that you defer for ten years is effectively cut in half. And during those ten years your PEA doubles twice.

Also, when we retire, some people assume that we will be in a lower tax bracket. (Actually, I hope not. I would rather retire rich and pay my taxes.) But we may find that some of our income is sheltered from taxes, and therefore any taxes that can be pushed forward could be paid when we are in that lower bracket. In heaven there are no taxes. Now, that's a low bracket we can look forward to.

Tax-deferred Retirement Accounts

Besides charitable giving and offsetting losses, we can also use tax-deferred retirement accounts to avoid taxes. Many investors have retirement savings in IRA accounts, 401(k) accounts, or Roth IRA accounts. We have concentrated on index funds because they are tax efficient and thus minimize taxes in our taxable account. What should you do when you wish to own something that is not tax efficient? For instance, if you need to sell some index funds and buy bonds, should you use the index funds in your IRA account or the index funds in your taxable account? If you sell index funds in your taxable account, capital gains taxes are due. Then, when you buy bonds, the bond interest will be taxed.

But if you sell the index funds in your IRA account, no capital gains taxes are due. And when you buy the bonds in your IRA account, the interest will be tax free. Therefore, whenever you wish to switch securities (or hold securities that are not tax efficient, such as bonds, stocks, or actively managed mutual funds), use the money in your tax-deferred retirement account.

Investment Expenses Are Tax Deductible

There are costs associated with earning the income in your taxable investment account. These expenses are deductible from your income before taxes are calculated. For instance, margin interest is a deductible expense. (More about margin in Chapter 27, "Margin Accounts.") As an example, if you earned $500 in dividends from your index funds, and you have $500 in margin expenses that year, then the dividend income is reduced by the margin expense, and no tax is due. This effectively eliminates the tax. Dividend income, interest income, and capital gains dividends can all be offset by your investment expenses.

Buying this book is an investment expense. Its price can be deducted from your investment income.

CHAPTER 17

Exit Strategies

When It Is Time to Spend Your Money, You Need to Consider Three Things

Your Time Horizon: When Will You Need the Money?
WE HOPE THAT YOU HAVE already given this some thought, but now the time horizon is changing. You are planning to retire, and you will want an income each year. Therefore, some of your money has a short-term time horizon.

The Volatility of Stocks Versus Bonds
   In Chapter 12 we looked at the short-term returns on the S&P 500 Index and concluded that we needed a long term to capture stock returns safely. But now we have a short-term time horizon, so we need to look at bonds and bills. For money that you will need in a few years, only bonds or short-term securities are appropriate.

The Possibility of Inflation
   Inflation causes the purchasing power of your money to decline. For someone living on a fixed income, inflation is a major risk. What can you do about possible inflation?

The Cost of a Mistake

Let's consider a retired couple with $850,000 in index funds. They want to withdraw $50,000 per year to live on. The stock market has been going up, and they do not want to pay the capital gains taxes that would be due if they switched to bonds, so they leave their money in the index funds so it can continue to grow at a high rate. But inflation rises and the market goes down. After five years they have withdrawn $250,000, the market has declined, and they have $500,000 left. Now they are probably sorry that they chose to remain in the stock market because their portfolio has shrunk, not grown, and they still have many years to live.

Brief moral of this story is: fixed income securities (bonds) protect your principle. Also, try to withdraw money when stocks are up, not down. So, if you are planning to retire and live off your investments, think about switching some money to bonds and think about timing the switch so that you sell before you need the money, hopefully when stocks are up.

Rolling Your Principle into Bonds for Retirement

For example, if you need a pretax income of $50,000 per year to maintain your lifestyle, and you calculate that you will be able to earn that if you put your money into 6% bonds, then you would need $850,000 worth of 6% bonds. If you have $850,000 in your PEA, you can sell your index funds and buy the bonds. You will guarantee yourself $50,000 per year until the bonds mature. When the bonds mature you can buy new bonds, and thus you have created a $50,000 income for life.

But, you will probably owe capital gains tax on the index funds. Let's say that your cost basis was $200,000, so the gain would be $650,000. The 20% tax would cost $130,000, leaving only $720,000 to buy 6% bonds, giving you an income of $43,200 per year. In addition, the interest on the bonds is taxable each year, further reducing the $43,200 per year income.

Fully converting our entire portfolio to bonds is secure, but the tax consequences of making the switch are very high. Also, you lose out on any future gains in the stock market, and you might be retired for thirty years. In thirty years each dollar in the stock market could become sixty-four dollars. Finally, your income is exposed to inflation.

Funding to a Time Horizon

Instead of investing $850,000 in 6% bonds to earn $50,000 per year for the rest of your life, an alternative strategy is to select a time horizon and fund to that date, leaving the balance in the stock market. We saw that since 1936 the average return over ten years was $1.00 becomes $3.38, the minimum was $1.05, and the high was $6.87. We want to leave some money in the stock market but still guarantee our income for the next ten years. The $50,000 a year for ten years could be satisfied by purchasing a portfolio of ten bonds, the first maturing in one year, the second in two years, and so on for ten years. Each year one bond would mature and the rest would pay interest. This portfolio of ten bonds would only cost $310,000.

For example, we purchase a $31,000 bond paying 6% and maturing in one year, and a second $31,000 bond paying 6% and maturing in two years, and so on until the tenth year. The bonds would cost a total of $310,000 and the annual interest would be $18,600 interest per year. Each year one bond would mature. Therefore, the total income per year would be $49,600 ($31,000 + $18,600 = $49,600).

Having created our ten-year string of bonds, each year thereafter one bond matures. To maintain our ten-year string of bonds, each year we would sell $31,000 of index funds and buy a new bond that would mature ten years later. This way we guarantee $50,000 per year of income, and we leave most of our money in the stock market. Since the bonds only cost $310,000, this leaves $540,000 in the stock market, hopefully doubling two times in ten years, and definitely deferring the capital gains tax due on those funds. Capital gains taxes would still be due when we sell the index funds.

Avoiding Taxes with Tax-deferred Retirement Accounts

Many investors have tax-deferred retirement accounts. If this investor had $310,000 of his total $850,000 in his IRA account, then he could use that IRA money to switch from index funds to bonds. This would eliminate the capital gains tax on selling the index funds, and it would eliminate the taxes on interest paid by the bonds. Since many of us have money in IRA accounts, we should be able to avoid large taxes when it comes time to switch a portion of our portfolio from stocks to bonds.

Timing Our Exit

But buying a ten-year bond each year for $31,000 from a $540,000 index fund portfolio sounds essentially the same as withdrawing $50,000 from an $850,000 index fund portfolio. Why do we fund our retirement with ten years of bonds if we are going to withdraw money each year? What is the difference between the $50,000 from $850,000 (6%), which we said was a mistake, and the $31,000 from $540,000 (6%) that we are recommending? The answer is that the market might be down for several years. If we own bonds that guarantee a $50,000 annual income each year for the next ten years, then, if the market goes down, we can afford to wait until the market goes back up to sell our index funds. We want to switch from stocks to bonds when the market is up, not when the market is down. By guaranteeing our income for the next ten years, we can eat three meals a day and sleep well at night when the market goes down. If we did not have a ten-year string of bonds, then we would be forced to sell stock every year to eat. That would force us to sell when we do not want to be sellers. Funding the next ten years of annual expenses with bonds maintains the long-term horizon that successful stock investing requires.

Remember the table showing the number of months of stock market decline and recovery in Chapter 11? The average market decline was thirteen months; the average recovery was twenty-five months; the total is three years. If the market remains down for three to five years we can afford to wait and buy our bonds when prices come back up.

But you'll tell me that we are now market-timing, trying to beat the market, that we should practice what we preach. My response is the same as when we were entering the market. We can improve our total return by not selling when the market is in a major correction. Our goal is to get out with an average return. You will know if you are in a major correction. Funding to a ten-year horizon should give you ample time to exit the market when prices are up, not down. What we do not want is to find that we have to withdraw our money on a certain day, and on that day prices are low. By allowing ten years, we expect to exit the market on an average day and earn an average return.

Each average year we will buy another ten-year bond. But if the market drops significantly, then we will wait until prices come back up before buying our ten-year bond. If we have to wait three years, then we will of course buy an eight-year bond, a nine-year bond, and a ten-year bond to maintain our ten-year string of bonds.

To test this market exit strategy, we used the ten-year total return graph shown in Chapter 10. The low spot on the graph is the worst ten-year total return since June 1936. From September 1964 to September 1974, the total return on the S&P 500 Index was 0.48%. The white line on the graph of ten-year returns shows the return starting on September 1964 and holding our investment for six additional years. As you can see, not selling when the market was down but instead holding onto the investment and selling later improved the return.

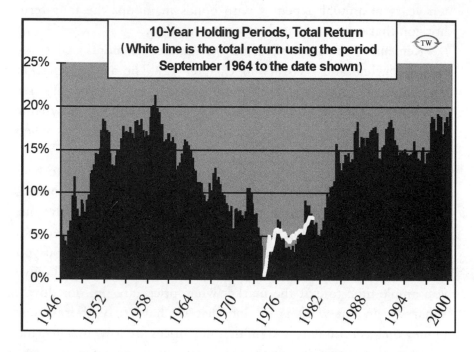

10-Year Holding Periods, Total Return
(White line is the total return using the period September 1964 to the date shown)

Now, we do not recommend trying to outguess the market when returns are average or above average. The difference between market timing and not selling when prices are down is a difficult concept to explain. The market timer is aiming for the highest returns. To get those maximum returns, the market timer tries repeatedly to enter and exit the market at the optimal moments. We are aiming for average returns. Our strategy is to hold the index for life. We try not to buy at the top by dollar cost averaging. When the market falls dramatically, we try to buy more if we are buyers and we have the money. If we are sellers when the market drops dramatically, we wait to sell until the market recovers.

Avoiding Mistakes

Why not just leave our $850,000 in the stock market and withdraw $50,000 each year, that is, a 6% withdrawal rate? As we explained above, if the market should go down, our portfolio would shrink. Then we would be withdrawing relatively larger amounts from a smaller portfolio. But, if we have the next ten years guaranteed with bonds, we have protected ourselves from short-term declines. By looking at history we observed that there have been no ten-year periods since 1936 with negative total return on the S&P 500 Index. In addition, we hope to avoid selling during a major market drop.

Therefore, we have funded ourselves to a rolling ten-year time horizon. By doing this we accepted some risk—that the market might go down for more than ten years. But the market has never stayed down for ten years before; therefore, we believe that is a reasonable risk. And we gain some potential return because we make money, if the market goes up, by leaving a portion of our money in the index funds.

Also, you have enough information to decide how many years you wish to fund with bonds. You may decide that five years of income protected by bonds is sufficient, leaving more invested in index funds. Or you may decide that seven years is sufficient. Or you may decide that protecting all of the next three years and half of the subsequent seven years will do. By looking at history, you make an educated guess about the future and then allocate your portfolio to bonds and stock accordingly. We saw in Chapter 11 that the average market decline and recovery has been thirty-three months and that 80% of the dips lasted less than eighty months.

How have we protected ourselves against inflation? The best hedge against inflation is making money. We expect the money left in the index funds to grow.

Growth Brings Benefits

We have just shown how we protected our income from a bear market by planning our withdrawals in advance and buying bonds. What happens if the stock market goes up while we are retired? Then the $540,000 left in the market continues to double. Approximately five years later we will be withdrawing $31,000 per year from a $1,000,000 portfolio. Instead of a 6% withdrawal rate, that is a 3% withdrawal rate. You will be in a position to give yourself a raise. That is inflation protection. If you live in retirement for twenty-five years, you could expect your PEA to double four to five times and become four to eight million. And this is your money. And you can still work part-time to supplement this income. This is not a government program with income limits.

Walter Morgan

Walter L. Morgan, who founded the Wellington Mutual Fund in 1928, was asked recently, "*What advice do you have for people considering mutual funds?*"

He replied, "If you're young, put most of your investments in common stocks. If you're over ninety-nine, not as much in stocks because you may not have much time to recover from market lows."[1] Mr. Morgan was ninety-nine at the time.

Mr. Morgan was directly addressing this concern. How much of your money should you leave in stocks, and how much should you put into bonds to allow your stocks to recover from market lows?

Action Plan

Almost everyone wants a simple plan to tell them what to do. Here it is. Decide how much annual income you are going to guarantee with bonds. Then each quarter, sell the correct amount of index funds and buy bonds. We could call this dollar cost selling.

Continue dollar cost selling as long as the market is making a new high or is within 10% of its high. However, if the S&P 500 Index is more than 10% off its high, then wait for the market to rise. When the market comes back up to within 10% of its high, sell enough stock to buy all the bonds that you had skipped while waiting. This will get you a sale price that is always at or near the high.

Summary

Now we have the whole picture. Get in to S&P 500 Index funds with an average or below average cost, defer and avoid taxes and expenses, earn the long-term market return, and get out at the high or near the high. As we showed in Chapter 3, this strategy beats all mutual funds. On top of this winning strategy, we add the endowment lifestyle. The endowment lifestyle increases our account balance and lengthens the time that we remain invested, allowing the larger balance to double again and again and again. When it is time to retire and secure an income from our endowment, we guarantee our near-term income with bonds and leave as much as possible in S&P 500 Index funds to continue deferring taxes and doubling. Since we have guaranteed our near-term income with bonds, we can wait out bear markets, and, therefore, we only sell our index funds when the market is at or near its highs. Because the money that we leave in index funds will continue to grow, we expect to raise our standard of living the longer we stay retired.

CHAPTER 18

Leaving Wealth to Your Heirs

HOW WILL YOU LEAVE YOUR WEALTH TO YOUR HEIRS? Two thoughts come to mind. First, not everyone handles wealth the same way. Second, there are no rules and few guidelines. So what will happen after you leave your wealth to your heirs?

If you have been teaching your heirs about the endowment lifestyle, then you will have seen how each heir handles smaller amounts of money. If each heir clearly understands that his or her long-term best interest is keeping his PEA growing, then you have the best indicator of future behavior.

When children are young, many parents encourage them to save by matching funds. For example, when our children would put $1,000 into their PEA, we would put in $2,000. This seems overly generous, but when measured by the effort required to save the money, clearly the children were making the bigger commitment. Also, it caused their account balance to rise rapidly, which had a motivating effect. Finally, it made a clear statement that we value saving and wish to encourage it. Since our children do what we do, setting an example where they can see it is important. Finally, children can understand the long-term goal, and parents should show clearly that the PEA is the beginning of lifetime wealth. The PEA is not for buying toys.

One rite of passage is switching from a custodial account for minors to a personal account at age twenty-one. My college-age son intimated that he would like to liquidate some of his account and purchase a two-wheeled vehicle. Of course, Mom and Dad had other opinions, but the key to success is to work through a transition as a team, not as antagonists. My reply was, "It's your account, and you can do what you want with it. But if you don't stick to the goal that it was set up for, then I don't have to put any more money into it."

The next big event is earning a living. If your heirs save their own money, you can be pretty confident that they will save yours when they get it.

Finally, there is record keeping. You may ask, "How will I know what my children did with the money that I gave them?" I have been assuming that giving the money includes the right to know how it was invested or spent. If you have a plan, such as this one in mind for their future, then you can work on having their PEA grow together. If the money is given to establish a PEA and you are matching deposits into a savings program, then watching the account grow motivates both parties. It motivates your heirs to save, and it motivates you to give again when you see your heirs investing wisely.

Some people are concerned that their heirs will not work hard enough if they have a lot of money. One nice thing about the endowment lifestyle is that people still need to have a job. The job pays for current expenses and debt repayment while the PEA grows larger if left undisturbed. Understood correctly, this motivates the heirs to work and allow their PEA to grow larger.

This is in contrast to either giving heirs money and seeing if they know what to do with it, or putting the money into a trust account until the heir is forty years old and then seeing if he or she knows what to do with it. Alternatively, some parents may purchase a business for their child or pay private school expenses for their grandchildren. All of these methods involve risk that the heir does not appreciate or manage the gift correctly. However, if your heir has management of his or her own PEA, he will make his own decisions, which creates a 100% involvement in the decision-making process. You may be training the spouses of your heirs, who have not had the benefit of learning about saving from you. Since everyone has to learn what to do and what not to do in life, it seems that the early lessons are the cheapest tuition. Training your heirs in the endowment lifestyle may cost a few dollars now, but it establishes a pattern of sound management that will ensure that when your entire endowment passes to your heirs they will know how to manage it.

Trust accounts are still appropriate for young heirs. But the key issue is training and education. If you can train your heirs to manage an endowment, then larger amounts of money should not create problems. Everyone can understand that if $10,000 doubles in five years, so will a larger amount. The key is keeping the principle invested and growing.

Chapter 19

What's Your Portfolio Management Philosophy?

Did you know that there is a debate between people who actively manage portfolios and passive investors who invest in the market indexes? To listen to either side there is little room for compromise. It is either an efficient market and you can't beat it, or all the profits go to those who hustle and the efficient market is baloney. We believe that both theories are right.

The Active Management Head-Trip

People have been actively managing portfolios of securities for years. When speaking with active fund managers, you will learn that they believe they are "adding value" and providing "incremental return." In fact, most active managers do not outperform the market averages, but the myth persists. For you it may be small potatoes to change your investment philosophy. But people on Wall Street have traditions to overcome. Please be prepared to be patient. Many savvy market professionals remain in denial about the benefits of index funds. The idea that you could outperform everyone else by earning the average return seems to be an oxymoron. Also, for an active manager to accept that the market average offers a superior return may mean admitting that they did not do so well in the past. Therefore, for an active manager to switch to indexing may invalidate his career, his belief system, his prior promises, and his self-image. In fact, we need the active managers because they make the market efficient. All their individual decisions to buy or sell based on the latest information create the efficient market that index investors enjoy. If active managers did not create an efficient market, then index investing would not work as well.

The Law of Large Numbers

Have you ever considered life insurance? Life insurance companies do not follow their policyholders around to see if they look both ways when crossing the street. How do insurance companies earn a living if they do not know when people will die? The insurance industry uses actuarial tables that indicate how many people of certain ages will die each year. Then the insurance companies simply price their life insurance policies to give them a profit after they pay the beneficiaries. Their only requirement is to insure enough policyholders so that no single individual can cause a big loss—essentially, what we call diversification.

But you and I are active managers when it comes to our own lives. We look both ways when we cross the street. We don't just say, "I can't beat the actuarial table so I won't bother to look before crossing the street." Not at all! We exercise, we take vitamins, and we go on diets. We are not looking for an average lifespan; we want to maximize our lifespan.

So while the law of large numbers works for the life insurance companies, active management works for us. Both philosophies are valid at the same time.

The same law of large numbers is at work in the U.S. stock markets. You can think of the efficient market theory as simply the law of large numbers. When a market is efficient, then large numbers of individual events will demonstrate average results, which are predictable over time. We can enjoy the benefits of the law of large numbers with index funds and minimize our costs. Others can actively manage a portfolio by trying to predict which company will merge, which company will increase sales, and which company will dominate the market. If they are right, they will earn profits from trading or investing. Both approaches are valid at the same time!

The only remaining question is, "Which kind of investor are you?" Please don't say, "A little bit of both." Either answer could be right, but a little bit of both will be successful at neither.

What could be successful is that you create two accounts, one PEA that you fund with index funds, and another that you use for active investing. If you do well at trading, great; that account will grow. But if you do poorly, take whatever is left in the trading account and transfer it to the PEA.

Besides this book, where we use equity mutual fund managers as a proxy for active investment managers, several studies have examined the results of individual investors trading their own accounts. In case you haven't read the research, most individuals who try trading lose some money and then stop trading. Some individuals lose a significant amount of their money, and a few individuals make a significant profit. Therefore, for most people the answer to the question "What kind of investor are you?" should be "A passive index fund investor."

CHAPTER 20

Do You Need a Broker?

STOCKBROKERS, FINANCIAL CONSULTANTS, TRUST OFFICERS, investment advisors, and financial planners provide a valuable service. Try measuring the cost of making a mistake against the cost of a financial advisor. Of course, you have to pay your financial advisor! You also have to pay for flying lessons. How would you like to fly a plane without a flight instructor? Would you recommend climbing a mountain without a guide? Why don't you fix your own car, or cut your children's hair? Have you ever tried doing your own plumbing repair? These are all things that you could learn to do. So why do you consult an expert for these services? The reason is that you don't want to face the cost of making a mistake.

What Does a Mistake Cost?

A friend of ours works for a large mutual fund company taking investor phone calls. He says that every time the market goes down a few investors call and sell all they own. Sometimes they even tell him, "I know I shouldn't be doing this, but I'm just scared."

Do you think those callers were following the advice of a market professional? How would you feel if you were out on a yacht when it started to rain and the skipper told you, "I've never been out in weather like this before; I'm not sure we're going to get home." At least when you set off, you trusted the skipper. That was wiser than taking the boat out alone. But what is missing on this boat? Experience.

The point is everyone needs experience. You have to get experience from someone. You could have learned from your parents. Or you could have started investing when you were young. Or you could have had a long relationship with your stockbroker. But no one is crazy enough to start investing without any experience. If you do not have experience, then you need an experienced counselor. It doesn't have to be a professional counselor that is paid for giving you advice, but you need to get advice from someone. If you don't have someone, then you must find someone.

When will you have enough experience to manage your investments yourself? Even experienced people discuss their strategies with other people. Even experienced investors read newspapers, magazines, and books about investing. You will have to decide when you know enough to manage your investments on your own. But don't stop calling your stockbroker just to save a few dollars.

Selecting a Financial Advisor

Now, your stockbroker may not have read this book yet, but he or she knows about index funds.

Why don't they sell this plan? Some do. Any stockbroker should be able to agree with the common sense of this investment plan, but he'll earn no commissions if you invest in no-load index funds. That is one reason the return is above average.

We get really worked up when someone who has read this book but does not understand investments comes back from his or her stockbroker and says, "I decided to put everything in stocks." Not that we believe stocks are bad. But it bothers us to think that someone went to a stockbroker and explained what was on his mind. And then, because the broker makes big commissions selling stocks, or because the broker believes in active management, he was persuaded to buy stocks that would clearly not fulfill his long-term goals as well as following this plan. So the moral of the story is, if you want to see this type of growth and returns with security in your life, you must take charge of your investment decisions. No one is going to give you money—just the opposite.

How would a good broker work for you? We recently asked that of a broker who told us that 30% of the assets that he manages for clients go into index funds. This individual worked on the New York Stock Exchange for many years. Six years ago he became a stockbroker at a major brokerage firm. His clients get the benefit of his twenty-five years of experience in the financial markets. When he puts a client's money into an index fund, it is not a "no-load" index fund. He uses his firm's index fund that charges higher annual fees, and he receives income from the money that he helps his clients invest. This is a fair exchange. You should pay him for helping you.

What should you look for in a stockbroker? Besides honesty you should look for years of experience. When you meet the individual, ask what experience he or she has. Expect to interview several stockbrokers before you select one that will work for you. If you are going to pursue the strategy in this book, ask him, "What do you think about putting most of your money into index funds for life?" If he responds that you can do better following his advice, then you have found out what you wanted to know. Keep looking for a broker because this one wants to actively manage your account.

Therefore, you will have to put this plan into action yourself. If you want a financial advisor to help you with your investments, you should expect to compensate that person. If the only way he can get paid is to sell you securities that earn him a commission, then he will not sell you no-load index funds, like the Vanguard Index 500 Trust.

Are you hearing a double message here? It's true; you need the financial experience of an experienced stockbroker to guide you, but you will have to tell him or her what to invest in. Normally, people who need help do not direct their brokers. But you can do it! Try giving them a copy of this book.

What can you do? You have two choices. Either manage your own investments or find a financial advisor who will work with you. Tell him or her that you want to invest in index funds and listen to his suggestions. If he fails to offer you any index funds after you have told him that you want index funds, then he isn't being straightforward. Find another advisor. Don't buy something that you don't want. Shop around for an investment advisor that you can work with. If you are going to invest for the rest of your life, then you can spend a few weeks or months researching where to invest. But start now.

CHAPTER 21

Why Not Buy Individual Stocks?

MANY OF THE THINGS THAT WE HAVE DISCUSSED apply to stocks as well as index funds, but not all. Many people will counsel you to invest in stocks. Let's review why we prefer owning an index fund to owning individual stocks.

First, buying individual stocks is like betting on a horserace; no one knows which stock will run the fastest or the farthest in the future. Second, to shed laggards and add winners to your portfolio requires attention. If you don't have the time or inclination or discipline to pay attention to the market, stick with index funds. Third, most individual investors and many brokers are in reality "buy and hope" investors. They buy a stock and hope it goes up. Is that your strategy? *Is that a strategy?* Fourth, active management requires at least three successfully executed trades: the buy, the sell, and the buy of something else. But investing for life only requires a single buy. Instead of "buy and hope," passive index investors are "buy and hold for life" investors.

Stocks Versus Index Funds

One advantage of stocks over index mutual funds is that there are no management fees; you are the manager.

Individual stocks may go up more than the market for a short period. But few stocks beat the market consistently for many years, and if one does, could you have identified it and purchased it before? And would you have put all your money on that stock? (Remember, if it were easy, everyone would be doing it.) But if we invest in an S&P 500 Index fund, we can say with certainty that we will perform like the market every year. Since our wonderful tax-deferred compound returns do not become significant until we have been invested for many years, we should pick our winner ten or twenty years in advance. Therefore, we cannot expect to obtain these returns picking stocks or buying an actively managed mutual fund. Why?

Why won't stocks be able to match or beat the index fund returns? (1) Because every time you trade a winning stock you must pay the capital gains tax which cuts into your compound returns. (2) If you are faced with a stock that is going down, and you have made money in the past, you will wait to sell until it really goes down, thereby hurting your average returns. (3) You must pay commissions and transaction costs to manage a portfolio actively. (4) Knowing which stocks will go up over the long term is a difficult game to win.

Warren Buffett's Track Record As a Money Manager

But some readers may say, "What about Warren Buffett?" Well, Warren has beaten the market during his lifetime. If you bought his stock twenty-five years ago, you would be doing well now. But do you want to bet your future on Warren Buffett? What will happen to the stock of his company when Warren is gone? Books are written about famous men after they become famous. By then it's easy to know which man is a winner. Try investing your money with a bunch of twenty-five-year-old money managers. Can you pick the next Warren Buffett?

Investment Vehicle Quiz

So, here is the quiz: Which would you rather pick to invest in for the rest of your life? (1) The next Warren Buffett from a group consisting of all twenty- to thirty-year-old portfolio managers? (2) The next Microsoft from a group consisting of the over 10,000 stocks trading in the United States? (3) The S&P 500 Index? Remember, to be fair about this, you have to put all your present and future savings on that choice.

Well, we counted your votes. It seems that everyone chose the index as the lesser evil. We never promised that you would like making money, just that we would show you how to make money. If you are wondering why index investing seems so unappealing, just think about the last time you went on a diet. Our human nature likes things that are illegal, immoral, and fattening. Our human nature also likes to spend money and gamble. An investment program that is safe, secure, and lasts a lifetime is about as exciting as watching a tree grow.

For the Hard of Hearing

For some readers the decision to buy index funds instead of stocks has been settled. But after people have read this manuscript, they have amazed us by their comments. So it is appropriate to list what works for stocks and what works for index funds. Remember, you have to make the decision of how much money to put in each type of investment.

What Techniques Work for Stocks?

If you buy a stock, hold it, and reinvest the dividends, you will get compound returns, the same as you would by holding an index fund. You will also defer your capital gain tax until you sell the stock. When it is time to retire, you can sell the stock and buy bonds. These concepts apply to stocks and index funds.

Diversification

Assuming that you have a stock in mind that will beat the market, do you want to put all your money on that one stock? But as soon as you begin to buy other stocks your returns start to become average. To remove the risk of only owning one stock, you begin to accept average returns. If you are going to diversify, why not accept the diversification of an index fund?

Market Declines

We have plotted the declines in the Dow Jones Industrial Average back to 1914, and the largest decline was 50% (except for the Depression). However, an individual stock can go down to zero. Many leading stocks have fallen 80% when the market average only fell 15%. Therefore, all assumptions that we made about market declines are not valid for individual stocks. All predictions about the future growth rate of your PEA are invalid when selecting individual stocks.

Long-term Investment Horizon

Staying invested for a long period reduces the volatility of an index portfolio. Staying invested for a long period does not reduce the volatility of one stock.

Dollar Cost Averaging

The mathematics of dollar cost averaging works the same for a stock as for the index, assuming that the stock goes back up. But how would you have felt about dollar cost averaging Western Union Telegraph or Woolworth? Western Union was a communications company, and Woolworth was a nationwide retailer, but they are both out of business now. Their stock prices were high once, but they fell and never came back up. When you dollar cost average an individual stock, you could end up buying more of a stock that is going down never to come back up. However, the entire market always comes back up.

Margin Limits

In Chapter 27, "Margin Accounts," we will demonstrate limits for margin borrowing that are based on actual historical movements of the Dow and S&P 500 indexes. Since a stock can go to zero, using margin with individual stocks is always speculative. However, with an index fund small amounts of margin borrowing are not speculative.

Stock Pickers

Perhaps the difference between buying stocks and index funds can be best demonstrated by looking at active fund managers. Before taxes and fees, the S&P 500 Index outperformed 86% of the equity mutual funds over the past fifteen years.

Now, mutual fund managers are paid to manage funds. They went to business school, and then they started working on Wall Street as clerks and analysts. They apprenticed under senior fund managers, and after years they were trusted enough to manage a fund. But even then their decisions are not theirs alone. They are part of a team with analysts who look at broad trends in the economy, analysts who compare market sectors, and other analysts who study financial statements and visit companies. There is also intense competition to beat all other fund managers by earning a higher return. Finally, because of their size, they pay smaller fees when they trade.

And then there is you. Can you outperform 86% of all equity fund managers using your personal investment strategy? Sure you can, sometimes. How about your broker? Can he or she outperform 86% of all equity fund managers? But 86% of the equity fund managers underperformed the S&P 500 Index. And we have not included taxes and fees. If we use after-tax numbers, the S&P 500 Index Fund outperformed over 93% of all mutual fund managers. Therefore, we have three strikes against us. (1) Most active managers don't beat the market over time. (2) We do not know in advance which ones will. (3) After taxes we do not get to keep all the returns from actively managed portfolios.

Risk Aversion

Let's not underestimate the value of boring. Risk aversion is normally worth money. That is why U.S. government bonds have the lowest yields, because they are the safest credit. The top 500 companies in the U.S. are a safer credit than any one company, or even a small group of companies. Therefore, the S&P 500 Index has superior credit compared to any individual company. But there are two kinds of risk. Credit risk—the risk of a company going bankrupt— is one type of risk. Market risk—price fluctuations—is another. The diversification provided by the 500 companies makes the S&P 500 Index less subject to price fluctuations than any single stock or any small group of stocks, such as a stock portfolio. Therefore, the S&P 500 Index has lower credit risk and lower market risk than investing in one stock or a small group of stocks.

How Does Low Risk Benefit You?

If you have a large sum in your Personal Endowment Account and decide to borrow to buy a house, leaving your money invested in index funds, would you feel just as secure knowing that your money was invested in a stock portfolio that you were in charge of managing? What level of comfort is there in the two choices? If you sleep well at night with significant financial commitments, it is because you have no fear for the future. The future of stock picking can't compare with the known track record of the market averages. Since your behavior is the biggest risk, choosing a strategy that lets you sleep well at night is important to your long-term returns.

High Returns with Low Risk

Index funds are an anomaly because they have the highest after-tax long-term total return and the lowest risk of any equity mutual fund or individual equity. How is this possible? That is why you are reading this book. Believe it or not there are some secrets on Wall Street that everyone in the crowd has not discovered. One secret is that the market average outperforms the market participants, and with lower credit risk and lower market risk. It is probably still a secret because it does not seem logical that the average could beat the best performers.

CHAPTER 22

Women and Children As Money Managers

THE INVESTMENT WORLD HAS BEEN VERY CHAUVINISTIC. If there ever were an example of an "old boy network," it has to be the people who manage money for the people who have money. Entrance into the club required that aspirants know where to find the door and pay the tuition to get in. Because active investment management requires experience, many people do not understand it. And the people who manage money for a living are happy to leave it that way.

Therefore, in many families women and children have been left out of the investment decisions. We all know that this is changing, but we also know that many women who find themselves single in midlife do not know how to manage their investments. And children—why, the idea that children could manage their investments has never even been considered.

But any high school student can understand the concepts in this book. And several have. After one student read this book, we received a phone call from his father that went as follows: "I don't know what has gotten into this boy. He never was interested in money, but he just asked me if he could take his $4,000 and invest it in index funds." Of course, we thought he should. But really, if the father in that family does not read this book, it may never happen. Understanding these concepts is not a problem for young people.

Fathers and mothers need to encourage their children to read this book because young people have the maximum investment horizon. A child who is born today can reasonably expect to live for one hundred years. Imagine how great compounding will work for them. Want to stop working when you're forty-five? Try investing when you are ten. A student that leaves college with $50,000 in his or her PEA at age twenty could expect to have $1,600,000 in his PEA by age 45 without adding another penny. If he continues to add to the PEA, the possibilities are staggering. Now, fast forward to age 70, 80, 90, or 100. What hath God wrought?

Women can easily understand the principles in this book. We do not answer all of life's questions, but most of the answers to financial questions are based on the fundamental principles presented here. And you now have enough information to question any advice that you may be getting from others. The secret to coping with unfamiliar responsibilities is to evaluate choices as they relate to your goals. In Chapter 5 the discussion of suitability remains the guiding principle of all investment decisions.

In addition, the life expectancy of a woman is seven years longer than a man's. Women, therefore, have a compelling reason to learn about personal finance. In fact, recent statistics indicate that women are already grabbing the financial reins.

From 1996 to 1998 the number of affluent women in the United States increased by 68%, rising from 8.8 million to 14.8 million women. During the same period the number of affluent men increased 36%, rising from 10.6 million to 14.3 million. There are 3.1 million women-owned businesses in the U.S. and only 1.4 million men-owned businesses. These are businesses with paid employees.

There is nothing male or female about wealth. Making your total wealth increase is about choices.

CHAPTER 23

Credit Card Debt

IN THE PERSONAL FINANCE COLUMN of the newspaper a reader asked, "I have extra money; should I invest it, or should I pay off my credit card debts?" The answer was to repay the debts first.

This may be good advice. It certainly is better to pay off a 16% debt than earn income at 8%. It is even better to live without debt.

But some people may experience temporary adversity. She may be a single mother with expenses on every side. What hope is there for the future? She has some money over and above the daily expenses. What should she do? To answer that question, let's assume that there is no extra money. Now, let's fast forward ten years, what will we find?

The answer is, what do we want to find? Do we want to have a PEA funded by a deposit ten years earlier? Or will that money, spent to reduce the credit card debt, be long forgotten?

One thing about daily life is that it is daily. You will always have daily expenses. You can have them with a PEA, or without a PEA. The beginning of your savings plan will be the beginning of getting out of debt.

To understand this concept, please remember Chapter 5 and the discussion of asset allocation. We said that we need multiple accounts—

credit card, checking, and savings—for the expenses of daily life and a Personal Endowment Account for long-term investments. The credit card debt is not long term in nature. Credit card debt comes under the allocation of daily expense accounts.

Viewed in this way, the answer is, no matter what, start a PEA for the long term. Some people always live with credit card debt. There is no reason that this should keep them from saving for the future. Personally, we believe that hope is the seed of success. Once a person begins to save for the future, repayment of debts will follow.

What is the fundamental principle in this chapter? Your PEA is for long-term wealth accumulation. Your daily life may generate extra income, may cost you as much as you earn, or may dip into the red. We see no contradiction in holding on to your long-term endowment while your daily life is costing more than you earn. There is always the hope that your financial situation will turn around soon. But what if it never does? What is the worst thing that could happen? You would end up in bankruptcy court. At that time, your index funds would be sold to pay your creditors, if not before. On the other hand, if your financial situation should recover, then you would have preserved your PEA and its future value.

If you want to motivate yourself to save more, several good books are listed in Appendix A. Also, credit-counseling agencies are available if your life is running in the red. These counseling agencies can extract concessions from your creditors to help you repay your debts within your budget, at no cost to you.

Credit Counseling Organizations

National Foundation for Credit Counseling
800-388-2277
www.nfcc.org

Myvesta.org (formerly Debt Counselors of America)
800-680-3328
www.myvesta.org

Debtors Anonymous
PO Box 920888
Needham, MA 02492-0009
781-453-2743
www.debtorsanonymous.org

CHAPTER 24
Classic Bond or Stock Allocation

THIS BOOK IS SPLITTING ALL THE OLD WINESKINS. A friend of mine is a trustee of a major university. He told me that the trustees were interviewing portfolio managers for the university's endowment. Four finalists were invited to give presentations to the trustees. He asked each the following question, "What would you say if we told you that we wanted 80% of our endowment in stocks?" All four gave the same response: "The recommended ratio is 40% bonds and 60% stocks."

Now, this may be your first book on investments, but you already know better than that. If the university planned to spend a certain amount of money in the next few years, we could recommend that they prepare for that disbursement by buying bonds. But if we go visit them thirty years from now, and they still have their endowment 40% in bonds and 60% in stocks, then they simply left money on the table. They could have earned higher returns in stocks, and with less risk. Finally, none of the four prospective money managers explained why they recommend 60% stocks and 40% bonds. Is it because they didn't want to say "I don't know"?

You will read in the newspaper that a well-known investment advisor has changed his recommended portfolio allocation of stocks to bonds from 60%/40% to 55%/45% due to uncertainties in the equity market, or vice versa. What are these people talking about?

The reason people want to own a portfolio of 40% bonds and 60% stocks is to reduce volatility. The thinking is that when the stocks decline in a bear market, the bonds will hold up the value of the portfolio. This is true. But, when the stocks go up in a bull market, the bonds will hold back the value of the portfolio.

How did we solve this problem? Perhaps naively, we stated that you should know your investment horizon. If you have more than ten years to invest, you can safely put your money into index funds (stocks) and expect to end up with more than you started with. Our index fund portfolio will be more volatile, but over the long term we will earn more. Second, we proposed the endowment lifestyle, which will enable you to keep your index funds for the long term without withdrawing your money.

One important thing about reducing the volatility of the university's portfolio is that the fund manager doesn't want to get fired. That was the reason for the interviews: the previous manager had lost the account.

And this is no small consideration for you. Your stockbroker may not want to lose your account because the market declines. Or you may not be able to sleep well if your account is invested in stocks and the market declines. So, while 60% stocks and 40% bonds will earn less over the long term, it will reduce the short-term volatility of the portfolio.

In summary, even the best money managers are using rules of thumb that they may not understand. There is no right or wrong answer to the question of how much to allocate to bonds and stocks. Just don't say, "Well I've got some stocks. I guess I should have some bonds." Decide for yourself, according to your goals.

What is a reasonable goal that would require the use of bonds in a long-term portfolio? A reasonable goal would be to earn a high income from investing in stocks, but reduce the short-term portfolio volatility by allocating some percentage of the money to bonds. If this is something that you wish to achieve, then 60% stocks and 40% bonds is how to do it. When stocks go down, the bonds will hold up 40% of the value of your portfolio. When stocks go up, then you will only go up 60%. If your participation in the investment process is opening your brokerage statement once a month and looking at the bottom line, then an allocation of 40% bonds and 60% stocks will provide growth with minimum fluctuations in the bottom line.

A second reasonable goal is uncertainty about your actual time horizon. What if you think that you might want to withdraw the money in your PEA sooner than you planned? If this is the case, reducing the volatility of the bottom line on your brokerage statement is in agreement with the uncertain nature of your investment horizon.

For us taxpayers, bond income is taxable while stock index funds accumulate tax deferred. So the penalty of owning bonds costs us more than it costs a nontaxable university. Also, we consider the bottom line on our statement history. Our eyes are on the future where things will happen to our total wealth. If we are looking far into the future, then short-term volatility does not concern us. But only we can say this, because we made the investment decision.

In the case of a board of trustees, if the members have not agreed to seek long-term returns, then 60% stocks and 40% bonds may be the correct allocation. This is not because it maximizes the total return, but because it minimizes complaints when the market goes down.

Therefore, what would we recommend for a university endowment? Once the trustees were familiar with these concepts, we would ask, "What is your long-term goal for the endowment? Will it be bigger, smaller, or the same size thirty, fifty, or one hundred years from now?" We predict the trustees will unanimously declare that it should be bigger. The second question is, "Do you plan to withdraw 40% from the endowment in the next ten or twenty years?" If the answer is no, then clearly an allocation of 60% stocks and 40% bonds is incorrect. They should put all of the endowment in stocks. Since most institutions have similar goals, and since most have allocated 60% to stocks and 40% to bonds, most are leaving money on the table.

CHAPTER 25

A Look Ahead

What If Everyone Read This Book?

PEOPLE OFTEN ASK ME, "Why doesn't everyone invest like this?" Or sometimes people say, "If everyone reads your book, it will change Wall Street."

If Everyone Read This Book, Stockbrokers Would Starve

People tell me that we wouldn't need as many brokers. But if everyone read this book, they would have more money. In the end, rich people call their brokers a lot more than poor people; therefore, Wall Street would grow, not shrink.

If Everyone Read This Book, the S&P 500 Would Become Overvalued

This may already be happening. The Vanguard Index 500 Trust has become the largest mutual fund. There were already 635 billion dollars invested in index funds in 1998. But even more is invested in what I call "closet index funds." That is, active fund managers are finding that they can't beat the index, so they join it. In other words, the active fund managers are quietly investing in the members of the

S&P 500 so that their performance numbers will not underperform the index.

If the S&P 500 Index does become overvalued relative to smaller companies, there will be two outcomes. First, the rich S&P 500 companies will buy the smaller companies, using their overvalued stock. Thus, the small companies will become part of the top 500, and their stockholders will see windfall profits. Second, traders will see those windfall profits and begin to invest in small stocks, causing a small stock rally. The small stock rally will cause dollars to flow from the top 500 to the smaller stocks restoring equilibrium.

If you own an S&P 500 Index fund during a small stock rally, you will be tempted to sell because the S&P 500 Index will be underperforming the small stock sector of the market. Be prepared, because this has to happen. But we know by looking at history that the leading 500 companies do very well if we stay invested for a long time. Whatever happens to us happens to everyone, because everyone owns a part of the market. We just ride through the turmoil more efficiently.

Finally, we are investing in the leading 500 companies in the U.S. Many things will change, but people will always have jobs. Some companies perform better than others; our strategy is to bet that the top 500 U.S. corporations will be the winners, not the losers.

If Everyone Read This Book, Stocks Would Go Up, Removing the Advantage of Owning Stocks

This should happen to a small degree. When the majority of investors understand how they can maximize their total wealth by investing their Personal Endowment Account in index funds, they will do it, and the prices of stocks will rise generally. This will benefit those investors who started early.

But will stock prices rise to a level where this plan is no longer advantageous? We think not, because the rest of the world is learning about capitalism and investing. The number of investors is increasing worldwide. Capital will flow to the leading companies. Millionaires in Manchuria will affect stock prices in New York. And there will always be growth in companies. As long as corporations are growing, and as long as more people want to get into the market, stock prices will continue to rise. Because of all the people in the world who are becoming wealthy and who are not participating in the market today, there seems to be a large supply of future investors.

Long term, relative to bonds, stocks will always return more. Stocks will always return more than bonds because of lifestyle risks. If our car breaks, we can liquidate a bond, but we may not be able to sell our stocks for what we paid for them. Also, stockholders assume the risks of profits and losses.

What If Social Security Allows Personal Investment Accounts?

Since the beginning of Social Security in the 1930s, the current workers pay the Social Security tax, which is then immediately redistributed via Social Security checks to retirees. Imagine how large the endowment would be if they had only taken 1% a year and invested it to create a Social Security Endowment Fund? But we must remember that in the 1930s everyone was suffering through the Great Depression, and they were not about to invest in stocks!

Recently, some lawmakers have proposed that each individual worker be allowed to manage a portion of his or her Social Security funds in his own account. As far as the stock market is concerned, a lot of little endowments would in aggregate be the same as one large fund. If each worker were allowed to manage only 5% of his own Social Security taxes, it would be equivalent to Social Security investing 5% of all its money in the market each year. This would quickly become the largest pool of capital ever created. What effect would this have on the stock market?

First, the stock market would become overvalued. Therefore, anyone who had invested before this big event would see windfall appreciation over time as the Social Security dollars became invested. This is already happening to some extent as more Americans invest through IRA and 401(k) retirement accounts.

Second, it might create a great period of prosperity, where anyone who had a new idea could find capital to start a business, and where American companies could expand overseas, buying companies all over the world.

Third, the returns on capital might become lower as more dollars chased the same amount of profits.

Fourth, it might increase market volatility as the whole population of the U.S. reacts to fickle public opinion creating larger bull and bear markets.

Finally, the only sure thing is that new dollars in the future will cause the market to rise. Therefore, investors today will bid up prices now if lawmakers begin to talk seriously about creating personal Social Security accounts. Therefore, investors who are in the market now, for the long term, will capture the long-term appreciation that these future dollars will create.

What Will Happen When the Baby Boomers Retire?

The concern that we have heard several times goes like this. When all the baby boomers stop saving for retirement and start spending their money, the market will go down. We don't know if this will or will not happen, but looking at the past, it seems relatively minor compared to the wars and depressions that the market has sailed through. Also, no one is asking about the women who work. The female baby boomers stayed home to raise their families, but the succeeding generation has two income earners in many families. In 1998, 67% of the population was employed, which is more than ever before. Therefore, there may be more workers saving for retirement than wage earners retiring even though the baby boomers stop working. Also, retirees do not spend their money all at once; they keep most of it invested so that they can generate an income for the next thirty years. Therefore, while the baby boomer generation will begin to retire in 2007, it is not clear that the stock market will go down. It is much more certain that desirable retirement property will go up.

What Will Happen If the Inheritance Tax Is Removed?

The Senate recently voted to repeal the inheritance tax. This would allow your PEA to pass to your heirs without taxation. In addition, the original cost basis of your investments would be forgotten. Combined with the principles in this book, a repeal of the inheritance tax would allow your endowment to compound from generation to generation. One look at the doubling table reveals what happens with a long-term investment horizon.

Chapter 26

Living for Giving

SOMEONE TOLD ME, "YOU ARE REALLY NICE. You are going to work all your life in order to accumulate wealth to leave to your heirs." I don't think of life in this light. I am not doing without things in my life to bless my progeny. I have discovered the endowment lifestyle, *and* I expect to teach it to my children. The main benefit that they will receive is starting early; it took me too many years to begin. Also, I am hoping that by the time I expire, my children will be ready to retire. In the meantime, they should get a good job if they wish to live well.

For me, wealth accumulation began with giving money away. When I was young, I wanted to make a million dollars. Then I came to know Jesus, the Son of God, and suddenly my life and my goals changed. Instead of wanting to make a million dollars, I wanted to give away a million dollars.

But you can't give what you don't have. Call me a philanthropist without money. Therefore, I gave what I had and believed that God would bless my giving. And He has.

In the twenty years since, my original goal has been fulfilled. So I began to seek another, greater goal. But what would that greater goal be? Giving more to charity?

With this book it has finally become clear. My next goal is to empower you to give away a million dollars. Would that satisfy you? If you don't have the money today, no problem; I didn't have any money either.

Some people say that they will give money away when they are rich. Forget about giving your money away when you are old! Give it away when you are young. Then you can see the fruits of your giving. Give when you don't have much. (It's cheaper.) To whom will you give your money when you're old? You would have to give it to some young person that you don't know. Get out today and find out who is doing good works. Help them. Support them. Become a benefactor. Start a good work yourself. Support an orphan, relieve a widow, visit the sick, and lend to the poor.

Just how much should you give away? The Bible clearly states that "The tithe belongs to God." If you don't give 10%, you are robbing God. Now, God is wise, patient, kind, long suffering, and merciful. He is not going to throw you in jail for robbing him. But He cannot bless you for it either. So, if you want God to "Open the windows of heaven and pour you out a blessing that you will not have room to contain," you can give 10% of your income in faith, believing that God will bless you, and He will.

As we mentioned before, the blessings of God are worth more than compound interest. "It is He that has the power to make wealth, and He adds no sorrow to it."

But what do you think God will say to the person who saves all his or her life, and then, when old, gives a million dollars to charities that he knows little about? How would you explain that to God? What is the chance that when they become old they never give anything away? Giving is a habit that starts when you are young.

So, give what you have today! Tomorrow you will have more. The blessing of God will be on your giving, and God will multiply the seeds that you sow.

I don't think that God is worried about our prosperity. Is it harder to give away a thousand dollars when you have nothing left, or when you have your PEA compounding for life? God might surprise us and say that the person with savings is just as generous, and somewhat smarter.

The key is giving today. Giving will even change you! For example, if you are giving charitably to please God, it is pointless to do something unjust or immoral to accumulate the wealth you will be giving away. How can you take advantage of one man to bless another, in the name of God? Or, suppose that you are tempted to be greedy. You cannot be greedy and give to charity; one act cures the other. And if you are greedy for the blessings of God and, in so doing, you give your money away, you will grow in faith.

Some may say that they cannot afford to give. But I feel that I cannot afford not to give. All my wealth comes from God. To continue to be a channel of God's blessing to others I must continue to give. If God uses me to bless others, he has to bless me first. And God uses me because I have given and will give again.

If you want to give more money than you possess, then you will be interested to learn that Jesus said: "No one who has left home or brothers or sisters or mother or father or children or fields for me and the gospel will fail to receive a hundred times as much in this present age (homes, brothers, sisters, mothers, children and fields—and with them persecutions) and in the age to come eternal life" (Mark 10:29). If you believe this, then you can receive one hundred times what you give to God. You can give money to charity believing that you are doing the will of God. Why not believe that God will bless your giving one hundred times so that you can give larger gifts in the future? You can't take your wealth with you, but you can send it on ahead through giving. Only what you do for God lasts for eternity.

Part 3:
Margin Borrowing and Advanced Concepts

CHAPTER 27

Margin Accounts

FOR MANY READERS OF THIS BOOK, advanced strategies are not necessary and will never be necessary. Advanced strategies require your complete attention. If you want to invest it and forget it, then you are a normal long-term investor. But, some people will use advanced strategies (for better or for worse, for richer or for poorer). Advanced strategies do not guarantee a higher return. Remember, even the pros haven't beaten the market averages consistently.

Why Margin?

We are going to discuss margin borrowing. Are you a sophisticated investor? If you are not sure, then you probably aren't. I recommend that you have an experienced investment advisor to help you manage your finances if you are going to employ leverage. My reasoning goes as follows: The cost of a mistake justifies paying an investment advisor. The increased probability of making a mistake while using leverage (and the increased speed at which mistakes occur) justifies the added expense, if only as an insurance policy against a thoughtless error.

In addition, some people presently use margin incorrectly. They are taking more risks than they realize. This section will serve to guide you into sensible leverage strategies. We do not recommend speculative strategies at any time.

What Is a Margin Account?

If you want a margin account you must request it from your broker. Not all investment firms offer a margin account. Most mutual fund companies do not offer margin accounts. Also, IRAs, 401(k)s, and custodial accounts for minors cannot be in a margin account.

In your margin account, you can borrow money against your securities. Initial margin requirements are 50% equity to total account value for most stocks, and maintenance margin requirements are 35%. For example, if you have $100,000 of securities, you can borrow $100,000 and buy more securities, giving you a total account value of $200,000. Your equity is the $100,000 that belongs to you. The equity to total account value ratio is then 50% ($100,000 equity/$200,000 account value = 50% equity to account value). If the new security goes up, you can sell it, repay the loan, and keep the profit. But if it goes down, then you sell it and, in order to pay off the loan, you need to sell some of your original securities. This is leverage: it works for you or it works against you. If you have no experience and you make a mistake, you could lose the money that you started with. For this reason, we do not recommend this type of speculative margin borrowing.

A little known detail is that margin requirements can be increased at any time. This is done to protect the lenders during bear markets. Therefore, if you are close to the minimum maintenance margin requirement, normally 35% equity to total account value, and the minimum margin requirement is raised to 50%, either you must add money to the account or you will be closed out. The securities in your account will be sold to repay the margin debt. Therefore, you cannot count on the margin rules remaining stable. When the market is giving you problems, the margin requirements may become harder to meet.

Someone may ask, "What is the difference between borrowing against securities and borrowing to buy a house?" When house prices go down, the mortgage lender cannot say, "The value of your house has gone down, please give me more money." Also, house prices typically rise and seldom fall. Stock prices are significantly more volatile than residential real estate.

Sensible Margin Borrowing

There are, of course, sensible people who do have margin accounts. Sensible margin borrowing can improve market entrance and exit strategies, and it is not unduly risky. For example, if you know that you will receive a bonus at year-end, but you wish to invest in the market today, you can borrow on margin and buy today, then repay the loan at year-end. Using margin in this manner does not create a permanent debt, and you may be able to take advantage of an opportunity to buy when the market is down.

Periodic Investing

Or you may wish to invest a fixed amount each month. However, drawing a check automatically on your household checking account could cause overdrafts. Therefore, you use a margin account to invest regularly, depositing your savings into the margin account each month. If there is any mismatch between the arrival of deposits and securities purchases, margin borrowing covers the gap.

A Convenient Line of Credit

You may also find that your margin account is more convenient than applying for a short-term loan from a traditional lender. For example, if you want to remodel your house, you may choose to pay your builder using margin debt. When the remodeling is completed, you can refinance your home based on its increased value, then repay the margin loan. This could avoid paying appraisal, title, and closing costs on a short-term loan.

Another Tax Deduction

Expenses incurred earning investment income are deductible against the income earned. For example, if you earn $500 in dividend income and you spend $500 on margin interest, you may deduct the $500 margin expense from the $500 dividend income as a cost of earning the income. Therefore, you eliminate the tax on the dividend income.

Sensible Margin Borrowing Limits

How would you know when to stop borrowing from your margin account? The two variables are time and risk. When will you repay the loan? And how much could the value of the securities in your account go down? We can answer these questions from our historical data. The largest decline since 1914 was 50% (excepting the Great Depression), seen in Chapter 11. If your equity to total account value ratio was 80%, you could survive a 50% decline.

For example, if you have index funds worth $80,000 in your account and you borrow $20,000 and use it to buy more index funds, then your equity is $80,000 and your total account value is $100,000. The ratio of your equity to total account value is 80% ($80,000/$100,000=80%). If the market declines by 50%, your account value will decline to $50,000. Your loan is then $20,000, and your equity is then $30,000; therefore, your equity to total account value becomes 60%. If we never want to go below 50% equity to total account value, then we can feel safe if we never borrow more than 20% of our account value.

The other variable is time. If we keep a loan of $20,000 outstanding at an interest rate of 10% per year, the following year it will be $22,000. After two years, it will become $24,200, and after ten years it will become $51,874. Since the lowest ten-year total return was 0.50%, our total account value would become $105,000 and the equity ratio would become 51% ([105,000–51,874]/105,000). Again, we will not go below an equity ratio of 50% if we restrict our borrowing to 20% of our account value.

The worst total return for a five-year investment in the S&P 500 Index was $1.00 becomes $0.60 (Chapter 10). In this scenario, our $20,000 loan would become $32,210, and our total account value would decline to $60,000. This creates an equity to total account value of 46% ([60,000–32,210]/60,000).

Using a somewhat larger loan, $25,000, in the worst five-year scenario would result in a 33% ([60,000–40,262]/60,000) equity ratio. This is below the minimum margin maintenance requirement of 35%. We would have to meet a margin call. That would require selling about $10,000 of our portfolio, reducing it to $50,000, and then repaying $10,000 of the loan, reducing the loan to $30,262. This would bring us back to a 39% equity ratio ([50,000–30,262]/50,000). In the future, when the market recovers to its original level by rising 66%, we would not return to our original portfolio value of $100,000. Instead, we would return to $83,300. The $10,000 that we liquidated to satisfy our creditors accounts for the missing $16,700.

The above examples are the worst moments for the Dow Jones Industrial Index since 1914, and the S&P 500 Index since 1936. Also, we used a high margin interest rate of 10%. We wanted to test the lowest decline and the lengthiest decline to see if our limit passes the test of history. In my opinion, borrowing less than 20% of your account value is safe, assuming that you will not need to sell your securities while the loan is outstanding and assuming that your account consists of S&P 500 Index funds. Borrowing up to 25% is relatively safe. Borrowing more than 25% of your account value on margin creates an insecure situation. These percentages are based on the highest value of your S&P 500 Index fund portfolio, since the declines that we used were all declines from market highs.

These limits are based on historical evidence. There is no guarantee that the market will perform the same in the future as it has in the past. Also, these calculations only apply to the Dow and the S&P indexes. If you buy a stock it could go down to zero. Therefore, do not apply these limits to other securities.

In the next two chapters, we will examine ways to sensibly improve your investment results using margin. Please do not feel compelled to try using margin in your PEA. You should understand that while the 20% margin limit is based on historical fact—and I believe it—I do not live with a permanent margin balance. Each year-end I pay off my margin balance. Does this surprise you? In summary, we are discussing margin, but we are not recommending margin for everyone.

CHAPTER 28

Compounding Plus

ONE CREATIVE IDEA THAT YOU MAY OR MAY NOT LIKE is helping your money compound with margin borrowing. We have recommended dollar cost averaging several times. In Chapter 27, "Margin Accounts," we said that borrowing less than 20% of the value of your index fund portfolio would not create an insecure situation, given the historical movements in the Dow Jones Industrial Average and the S&P 500 Index. Combining these two ideas, we can propose a strategy that should help your PEA grow faster.

If we borrow 5% of our total portfolio on margin each year and reinvest it in more shares of our chosen index fund, we will supercharge the rate of compounding without creating a large margin debt. For example, if your PEA has increased to $50,000, then 5% is $2,500. You could begin an automatic investment plan that invests $200 each month, borrowing the money on margin. At the end of five years your margin loan would be $13,465 (using an interest rate of 10%), which is 26% of your original portfolio value. But if your portfolio had doubled, $13,465 is only 13% of a $100,000 market value. Also, the additional purchases will cause the portfolio to grow faster.

When do you have to repay this loan? As long as it does not grow too large, the answer is never. Think of your $13,465 loan compounding at 8% to 10%. Then think of your $100,000 portfolio compounding at 12% to 15%. Over the long term, the portfolio value will grow faster than the loan.

Loan Limits

To survive over the long term, you have to pass through several short terms. Therefore, we never want to see our loan grow to more than 20% of our highest portfolio value. For example, if the highest value of our portfolio were $100,000, then our limit would be $20,000, or 20%. If the value of our index fund portfolio declined to $80,000, the $20,000 loan would be 25%. This is not a problem since we are measuring our loan against our highest portfolio value ($100,000), because we are invested in an S&P 500 Index fund and we are basing our calculations on the historical total returns on the S&P 500 Index since 1936.

If the market continues to go up, the limit will never be an issue. What happens if the market goes down or flat? One could borrow 5% for three years and then the fourth year would bring the total loan above 20%, with interest. In this case you should stop borrowing. Cancel your automatic investment program. This is a simple remedy. Therefore, there is not much risk in using limited margin borrowing to increase the growth of your portfolio. The only additional requirement is understanding margin borrowing and paying attention to the size of your margin balance.

Borrowing is not regulated. There is no speed limit on debt accumulation. You can borrow more than your limit, but then you are speculating. You may not realize it until the market turns down, but margin loans greater than 20% of the highest value of your index fund portfolio are clearly speculative and hazardous to your wealth.

CHAPTER 29

Using Margin As an Exit Strategy

THIS IS AN ADVANCED STRATEGY that you may not want to use and that you may not even understand. It is not part of our central premise.

One nice thing about borrowing money is that it is not taxable. If I sell $10,000 of my securities, then a capital gains tax is due. But if I borrow $10,000 against my margin account no tax is due. What if I never pay back the loan? Wouldn't it be nice if we could live on borrowed money? If my portfolio is growing at 12% per year, and I borrow 4% a year, would my debt ever grow larger than my portfolio?

Let's put that another way: If a farmer has one hundred rabbits that multiply at the rate of twelve rabbits per month, and he eats four rabbits per month, will he ever eat all his rabbits? Even if a wolf comes and destroys fifty of his rabbits so that he only produces six rabbits a month, the farmer should still be able to harvest four rabbits. But now let's say this farmer has been going to a restaurant and borrowing rabbits, not eating his own. He does so because he realizes that his nest will produce more if he doesn't eat them. But his tab at the restaurant has been compounding, and after five months he owes twenty-five rabbits, but his nest has doubled to two hundred rabbits. As long as he is wealthy, he never has to settle the bill. Also, since he never sold a rabbit, he pays no taxes. Finally, with two hundred rabbits, harvesting four a month is only a 2% withdrawal rate, so our farmer's risk decreases with time. Life should be so simple.

Except for the wolf, it is that simple. How can we protect against the wolf? Our farmer has forty rabbits in the deep freeze. If his tab at the restaurant grows too large, he will eat his frozen rabbits while he waits for his nest to grow. In Chapter 17, "Exit Strategies," we discussed funding to a ten-year horizon with bonds. If you have ten years of income protected with a bond portfolio, then you should be able to wait out down markets.

When we discussed using margin to increase your compounding, we found that if your margin loan was growing too large, you simply stopped borrowing. But, if you're living on the borrowed money, then the remedy is not so simple. You can't just stop eating. You must have provided sufficient income in advance.

In Chapter 27, "Margin Accounts," we set 80% equity, or 20% margin debt, as a limit. If your margin debt grows to 20%, it is time to start eating your frozen rabbits. I hope you prepared a supply.

Small Margin Debt

Here is an example of borrowing 4% a year from your portfolio. If you have $100, then the first year you would borrow $4.00 and owe $ .40 in interest (@ 10%), and the year-end margin balance would be $4.40. The second year you would again borrow $4.00 and owe $ .84 in interest. Your margin debt would now be $9.24 ($4.40 + $4.84). The margin debt does not need to be repaid; it simply increases.

What would have happened in some of the worst markets of the past if we had been borrowing $4 a year with a starting portfolio value of $100? We will use rows from the table on stock market risk in Chapter 11.

High Date	Low Date	Max. Decline	Avg. Decline	Down Months
1/11/73	12/6/74	-45.1%	-33.4%	23.1

The decline that began on 1/11/73 was 45% in twenty-three months. If your initial margin borrowing were zero, your index funds would decline from $100 to $55; your margin balance would now be $9.24, and you would have an equity to total account value ratio of 83% ([55–9.24]/55). The 83% is a modest ratio given that the market would be at a historic low.

If your margin loan were $20, you would be eating frozen rabbits, your loan would grow to $24.20, and your portfolio would shrink to $55 giving an equity to total account value ratio of 56% ([55–24.20]/55). This would not cause you serious problems either.

High Date	Low Date	Max. Decline	Avg. Decline	Down Months
3/10/37	4/28/42	-52.2%	-33.3%	62.5

If the decline took five years and went down 52%, your account value would decline to $48, your margin balance would be $26.86, and your equity to total account value ratio would be 44% ([48–26.86]/48), starting from a loan of zero. This is much lower than we like but still above the maintenance margin limit of 35%. You should stop borrowing when the loan balance gets to $20.

If your starting loan value was $20, after five years it would become $32.21 without additional borrowing, and your account value would be $48, giving an equity to total account value ratio of 33%. This is slightly below the minimum maintenance margin limit; you would have to meet a margin call.

In our analysis of total return, the minimum ten-year total return was 0.05% from September 1964 to September 1974. Starting at $100, our account value would grow to $100.05. If our loan were zero we could borrow $4 for three years and then eat frozen rabbits, and the loan would grow to $37.16. This would give us an equity to total account value ratio of 63% ([100.5–37.16]/100.5). If we started the period with a loan of $20, it would grow to $45.00. This would give us an equity to total account value ratio of 55% (100.5–45.00]/100.5).

So, borrowing 4% per year is not risk free. That is why we need a bond portfolio, so that we can live on our bonds and not have to borrow more money against our stocks when the stock market is down. Using the worst declines in history, our limit of 20% margin and ten years of income guaranteed by bonds brings our portfolio through without serious harm.

These examples used the worst markets, not because we are pessimists, but because we want a plan that survives in the worst weather. If we know that we can survive the worst, then we can be optimists. What happens if we do not experience the worst decline in history?

Then your account continues to grow while you eat with other people's money. The account continues to compound tax deferred. When you finally die, your margin debt will be subtracted from your total portfolio value, and the balance will pass to your heirs. And that balance will be larger than if you had been eating your own rabbits.

You may think that borrowing 4% a year is a trivial amount. But taxable bonds that pay 6% interest return 4% after taxes of 33%. To summarize, if the market does poorly, we avoid borrowing. If the market does well, then we can borrow and increase our total wealth.

Summary

This concludes our strategies. It is clear that one can buy an index fund, hold it for life, and never pay any taxes at all on the growth or the income. In addition, by borrowing you can support your lifestyle in retirement, tax free. Also, while you are accumulating wealth, you can use other people's money to eat cake and allow your cake—your PEA—to grow undisturbed. The rich can have their cake and eat it too.

The nice thing about this growth is that it is predictable. You can match your human capital (future goals and future income) to your future PEA. It is also nice to know that you will beat the market, without even trying.

CHAPTER 30

Mistakes You Don't Need to Make

WE WOULD HATE TO CALL THIS CHAPTER "Mistakes That I Have Made," but we could. These reasons explain why you need an experienced investment counselor.

Selling When the Market Was Down

When my mother died, she had been managing my grandmother's portfolio with the help of a good, experienced broker. The portfolio was full of bonds, and the bond prices were all down because interest rates were high. I looked at the bonds, looked at their market prices, and said to the broker, "We will sell all these losing investments; from now on I will manage this portfolio." He objected and told me that the market would go back up, and therefore I should not sell at the bottom, but in the end he followed my instructions. Now I know that he was right and I was wrong. What is the lesson? (1) Don't sell when prices are down. (2) Recognize someone who has more experience than you do. And try to learn from him.

Staying Out of the Market Because It Might Go Down

You know about our having to pay for a house after the crash of 1987. Then I was sure that the market would go down again, but instead it has gone up ever since. It took until the 1990s for me to believe that it might continue to go up. Talk about uneducated. I had no sense of history, so how could I possibly know whether the market would go up or down? Therefore, you should study the tables on market movements until you have a sense of how the market behaves. Lesson: History teachers are right; those who don't study history are destined to repeat it. Since most investors can have only their personal experience to rely on, you can steal a march by doing some simple homework.

Buy a Stock and Watch It Go Down

My stockbroker recommended and then sold me a stock. I bought shares at $10 and it went to $13, then it went back down to $10; But my broker said, "Keep it; it will go back up." At $8 he said, "Keep it." At $3 he still said, "Keep it." In the end I got a worthless stock certificate. The moral of this story is: Recognize someone who has more experience than you, but don't believe everything they say. At some point you have to follow your own feelings.

Buy Something That Is Too Risky

I overheard someone saying that Teledyne stock would go up; therefore, I bought some stock. Each day on my lunch break I would watch the ticker tape in the window of the Merrill Lynch building. The first day I was up $900. The next day I was down $600, then up $1,300, then down again. These ups and downs actually upset my stomach. By the end of the week I sold and was glad to get out. I wish I could say that was the last risky thing that I ever bought. Lesson: Owning investments that you can live with is important. Don't overestimate your ability to live with risky (volatile) securities.

Try to Make Money As an In-and-Out Trader

After figuring out that some stocks go up and down all the time, I realized that I could buy when they are down, sell when they are up, and pocket the difference. My wife said that the company she worked for went up and down between sixteen and twenty. And she was right; it had been. So when the stock was around seventeen, I would buy it, and when it was around nineteen, I would sell it. But, there was usually a spread of 50 cents between bid and ask, plus commissions of about 50 cents per share on either side, plus taxes if I made any money. Then subtract any mistakes or miscalculations that I might introduce. Finally, I realized that it wasn't worth the effort; I was risking my money buying something that might go down and making hardly any profit. Lesson: Commissions, transaction costs, miscalculations, and taxes add up quickly the more transactions you make.

Buy Something Because It Will Lower Your Taxes

My brother and I split a share in a tax shelter totally on word of mouth. Someone, who knew someone, said it would be a great investment. The only way it lowered our taxes was that it was a total loss. Losing money does lower your taxes. Lesson: Tax benefits are fine, but you need to understand how you are going to make money. Second, if you don't know what you are getting into, you are trusting blind luck. It is amazing how people who will comparison shop a refrigerator will invest $10,000 on word of mouth. The promoters had a document an inch thick, but it was all projections of what would happen in the future. Were we well informed because we knew what they promised they could do? We should have asked to see what they had done in the past.

Believe Someone Who Tells You That He Can Earn You a Fortune Quickly

How many times has a broker promised that he or she has a system or strategy that is guaranteed to succeed? Fortunately, I didn't have enough money to follow every one. Those that I did listen to got me into enough trouble. In later years I began to ask, "Where is your evidence?" or "Can you show me your track record?" They usually would reply that their strategy was too new to have a track record, but it had been working great for the past six months. Lesson: There is a sign in the post office, "If it is too good to be true, it probably isn't."

Brag About Your Investment Success

Don't do it. Maintain a low profile. People won't love you any more because your investments are doing well. Some will love you less because no one likes braggers. If you do attract any friends, it will be for the wrong reasons.

Think Too Much of Your Investing Skills

If you look for the common thread in all these mistakes, the fault was lack of experience. I had no idea of what I was getting into, and I had no one with whom to discuss the probability of my investment success. In short, guys don't ask for directions. Lesson: You will pay tuition for investment experience. You can either pay a reasonable fee to an experienced guide, or you can pay by making mistakes.

Summary

Having made these mistakes, my wish is that you should not do the same. The strategy that we outline in this book is not risky. It has been clearly explained and you can invest with hopes of success that are based on historical facts. You should also understand what you are doing and why you are doing it, so that when your goals change, you can adjust your strategy.

But we realize that we may be leading some of you out of a quiet life and into the jungle of Wall Street. The reason is that the stock market has been producing superior returns. But not everyone on Wall Street is capturing those high returns. Many are underperforming by making mistakes. The strategy in this book keeps you from making all the mistakes listed above.

CHAPTER 31

Wall Street's One-Way Streets

WHEN YOU DECIDE TO INVEST FOR THE REST OF YOUR LIFE, decisions that you make today could affect you for years to come. Sometimes you can enter into a transaction today and not realize that it will be expensive to get out of it tomorrow.

Home Mortgages

Mortgage interest payments are generally tax deductible. But if you own a house without a mortgage, getting a mortgage and using the proceeds to invest is not tax deductible. The IRS differentiates between someone who gets a mortgage to buy a house and someone who mortgages his house for another purpose. According to the tax regulations, only the "acquisition cost plus $100,000" is tax-deductible. Acquisition cost is the price you paid to buy, build, or reconstruct the house. If you already own the house, taking out a mortgage is not financing its acquisition. Therefore, if you have paid off your mortgage, you may want to buy a new house with a mortgage, then take the proceeds from the sale of your old house to invest. If you are considering paying off your mortgage be aware of this restriction.

IRA and 401(k) Retirement Accounts

Contributions to an IRA or 401(k) plan are made with pretax income; interest and dividend income and capital gains are not taxed in an IRA or 401(k) plan. Withdrawals are taxed at your income tax rate when you make the withdrawal. You may begin to withdraw your money from these plans at age fifty-nine and a half, and mandatory withdrawals must be made starting at age seventy and a half. If you die with money in these plans, the income tax is still due and must be paid by your estate.

Roth IRA

A normal IRA is funded with pretax income. The Roth IRA is funded with after-tax income, but you will not pay income taxes when you withdraw the proceeds at age fifty-nine and a half. And there are no mandatory withdrawals at age seventy and a half. Also, if you die with money in a Roth IRA, your estate will not have to pay the income tax that would be due on a traditional IRA.

How Much to Invest in Tax-deferred Plans

How much should you invest in a Roth IRA, a regular IRA, or a 401(k)? If your employer is matching contributions to a retirement plan, you should contribute and obtain the contribution match. The total return on free money is hard to beat. The Roth IRA is more desirable once you are retired because neither withdrawals nor income and trading within the Roth IRA account are taxed. Regular IRA withdrawals will be taxed; therefore, you should avoid putting too much of your wealth into a regular IRA, if practical. You can convert regular IRAs to Roth IRAs by paying the tax now if your income is less than $100,000. If your employed income is greater than $100,000, then you may be able to plan to convert to a Roth IRA after you retire and your income is lower. Because the eligibility rules, the offerings at your job, and your age all vary, there is no single right answer to the question. But with the information you have in this book, you should be able to project where you will be in the future. If you plan to switch a portion of your wealth into bonds, it would be advantageous if that portion of your retirement savings were in a tax-deferred retirement plan. Beyond that portion, index funds are almost tax-free, and the money is yours without restriction.

Margin Borrowing

Some brokerage firms will allow you to margin index mutual funds, and some will not. Generally, if you cannot buy a mutual fund through a broker, they will not margin it. Therefore, if you plan to use margin, check with your broker to see if he will margin the securities that you wish to own.

Purchasing Index Funds

Some mutual fund companies wish to discourage day traders in their index fund, and therefore do not permit customers to call and invest on the same day. Instead the investor must mail in new investments. But several brokerage firms sell the same mutual funds and allow investors to purchase the mutual fund with a phone call. You may decide that paying a fee to the broker is worth the convenience of same-day execution.

All firms that sell mutual funds have a cut-off time for same-day trades. Do not expect to purchase a mutual fund for that day if you call late in the day. If you are going to be purchasing the same mutual fund on a regular basis, ask in advance how late you can place an order.

Most no-load mutual funds companies do not charge a fee for purchasing their mutual funds. But a broker may charge to purchase the same mutual fund. The broker may offer other useful services such as margin, same-day execution, and all your securities and record-keeping on one statement. You can always purchase a mutual fund from the mutual fund company for no fee and then transfer the shares to your broker, thus saving the fee.

Automatic Investment Plans

Mutual fund companies typically do not have margin accounts, but they do have automatic investment plans. Brokers have margin accounts and automatic investment plans, but they may charge a fee to buy the mutual fund that you desire. You can have the mutual fund company draw a check on your margin account and invest automatically. In this way your automatic investments are free and effectively written against your margin account at the brokerage firm.

What Not to Do with Debt

Guess what? After presenting these ideas, more than one person has asked, "The credit card company is offering me a loan at 3%; should I borrow money from them to invest in index funds?"

The short answer is an emphatic "No." But why? What is the difference between borrowing to buy a car when we could pay cash and borrowing to invest when we have nothing? If you don't have a PEA containing index funds, why shouldn't you borrow to start one?

First, the credit card company is only offering a 3% rate for a short term. They are planning to make money in the future—from you. Somewhere in the fine print it will say that after six months or nine months the rate will rise from 3% to 18%. That would leave the borrower in the unprofitable position of borrowing at 18% short term to earn 12% to 15% long term. Or when the rate rises, you could sell the index funds and repay the loan; but since the time horizon of the 3% loan is short term, the market might have gone down. So this strategy could end up costing money.

Second, there is no growth here. We want our total wealth to grow, but this transaction creates a debt that is equal to the amount of index funds. This means that any decrease in the value of the securities or increase in the cost of borrowing will create a losing transaction.

Third, we only invest in safe transactions when unexpected events will not disrupt our plans. We all have lifestyle risks. Imagine if you borrow $10,000 and then the interest rate goes up, the stock market goes down, the temperature drops, and you suddenly need to buy a new furnace that costs $4,000. If your stocks are worth only $8,000 and you sell $4,000 to fix the furnace, that leaves a $4,000 portfolio and a $10,000 debt. You have effectively borrowed against securities, which is similar to margin borrowing, and your debt to equity ratio is zero equity and 100% debt.

There is a proverb, "It takes money to make money." The plan outlined in this book borrows to avoid spending the money in our PEA. We borrowed when we could have paid cash, but we chose to use someone else's money to allow our PEA to continue growing while deferring taxes. But borrowing before we have any money creates debts that we cannot repay. That sends our total wealth in the other direction.

We recommend borrowing against items that provide their own collateral, such as a house or a car. And our debts should be smaller than our PEA so that our total wealth grows.

Borrowing to pay for college is an apparent contradiction. But the college graduate expects to graduate and begin working, which creates a new source of income to repay the college tuition loan. In addition, the college loan that we suggested was actually backed by parents who had the money to pay the tuition. Do you have parents standing by to cover your lifestyle risks?

Another person suggested borrowing $20,000 for thirty years from a bank, and at the end of the thirty years it would become one million dollars. But a person who does that starts out with a debt of $20,000 and index funds worth $20,000, with a total wealth of zero. Expecting to parlay zero into a million is a high-risk gamble. Instead, what we recommend is that you save your own money. If you can imagine repaying a $20,000 loan, then skip the loan and add to your PEA each month. Then your own $20,000 will grow to a million in thirty years. That is a low-risk strategy. Along the way, you can purchase items that you need with other people's money, and this will preserve your PEA, allowing your own money to compound undisturbed. If we only borrow to purchase items that have their own collateral, such as cars or houses, then we can always sell the asset to repay the loan, leaving our PEA intact.

CHAPTER 32

Which Index Fund?

SINCE INDEX FUNDS HAVE BEEN SUCCESSFUL for many people, the number of index funds has proliferated. In addition to index funds on the S&P 500 Index, there are index funds on the Dow Jones Industrial Average, the whole U.S. stock market, small cap stocks, bond index funds, emerging markets, Europe and Asia indexes, individual country indexes, global stock indexes, and several more. Each month a new index fund type is introduced. How can anyone keep up? We will post information on new choices and new research on our web site, www.total-wealth.com.

What index should you invest in? To answer that question we go back to our suitability principles. What is your time horizon? The time horizon that we have chosen is buy and hold for the rest of our life. Therefore, we are looking for a long-term solution. Fortunately, the S&P 500 Index has a long history and, since we can see what has happened in the past, we know what to expect.

Many of these new indexes have no relevant history. For example, an index of emerging markets, by definition, has no history. Also, international indexes contain currency exchange rates. When you buy a fund that invests in Japanese stocks, if the dollar/yen exchange rate changes, it changes your return. Since currencies are volatile, introducing foreign stock investments into your portfolio introduces volatility. Currency exchange rates have no positive long-term return because currencies are a zero sum game: what one currency loses another gains. Therefore, buying international indexes introduces more volatility (risk) without introducing more long-term return. Moreover, the members of the S&P 500 Index, are all selling their products globally. Colgate sells toothpaste in India. Boeing sells jets in China. Microsoft sells software in Argentina. We prefer to let the executives of these companies manage the foreign currency risk. Bottom line: The S&P 500 Index is globally diversified yet with low risk and a positive long-term return, and their stockholders get dividends in U.S. dollars.

When it comes to the American market, should we invest in the S&P 500 Index or a small cap index, or the total stock market of five thousand stocks? If you think back to your high school class, would you rather invest in the whole class, or just the leaders? Funny, but we all chose the leaders. In fact, research has shown that during some periods small cap stocks outperform the large cap stocks (S&P 500 Index members), but not often. Therefore, investing in minor segments of the market becomes a market timing game, which is inconsistent with our long-term buy and hold strategy.

In summary, the S&P 500 Index will not outperform all the other sectors of the world market every year. But, being in the right market on the right year is not the investment style that we have chosen. If we must pick one sector that will perform well over a ten- to thirty-year horizon, then the S&P 500 Index qualifies. It qualifies because we have sixty years of history to predict how it will behave. It qualifies because the S&P 500 Index is 69% of the total market value of all U.S. stocks, therefore investing in the S&P 500 Index is investing in the United States.

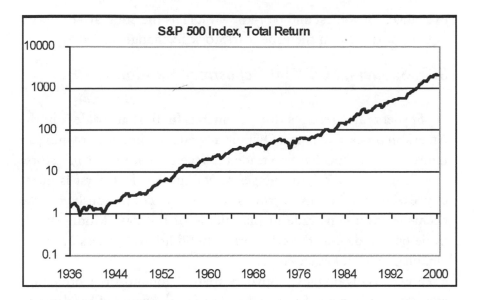

S&P 500 Index, Total Return

In this logarithmic chart of the Total Return on the S&P 500 Index since 1936 note that the slope of the line is relatively constant. This is what long-term investing in the S&P 500 Index will bring, almost constant growth.

Second, the Dow Jones Industrial Average should continue to perform with the S&P 500 Index. Beyond these two, we have scant evidence at present that any other market sector will definitely out-perform these two indexes.

Upcoming is a table of S&P 500 Index funds.

Exchange Traded Funds

But first we must mention Exchange Traded Funds (ETFs.) These are mutual funds that are traded on an exchange. A normal mutual fund is called an "open-ended" fund. If someone wants to buy it, the manager receives the investor's money and issues new shares. By contrast, investors trade shares in an ETF on an exchange. The oldest and best-known ETF is the Standard & Poor's 500 Trust traded on the American Stock Exchange, called Spyders.

SPY, Spyders, S&P 500 Depository Receipts

Spyders are receipts for an index fund that trade on the American Stock Exchange. Owning a Spyder is similar to owning an index fund, except that you trade the receipts with other investors.

There are several advantages to trading Spyders. First is intra-day execution. Because Spyders are traded continuously on the exchange, you can trade in the middle of the day. Mutual funds trade once a day, at the close price. In addition, Spyders are marginable at all brokerage firms.

Some disadvantages to Spyders are that you must pay brokerage commissions to trade Spyders. In addition, the value of Spyders can vary slightly above or below the value of the S&P 500 Index at the same moment. Typically, Spyders sell for slightly more than they are nominally worth. Also, there is a bid/ask spread to consider. Finally, the reinvestment of Spyder dividends is not automatic. You must instruct your broker to receive the quarterly Spyder dividend and then buy more Spyders. Some brokers are not able to do this for you. (You should check with your broker before you purchase Spyders.) With an index mutual fund, the dividends are automatically reinvested as companies pay dividends.

When all the pluses and minuses are added up, Spyders compete well with the best index mutual funds. Spyders are one-tenth of the price of the S&P 500 Index. Therefore, if the S&P 500 Index is 1,300, one Spyder share will cost $130. The annual expense ratio on the Spyder trust is 0.12%; the trust is managed by State Street Global Advisors.

Most people buy and sell Spyders to speculate on the market. But we would buy Spyders and hold them, reinvesting the dividends in more Spyders.

Because prices change, confirm the costs (expense ratio, front-end load) with the mutual fund before you invest. In addition, some funds have Redemption Fees. The redemption fee is charged to discourage in and out trading by shareholders. It is withheld if you sell quickly, but normally the redemption fee declines to zero the longer you remain invested.

In Descending Order by Total Return

A quick glance down the "3-Year Return" column shows that not every S&P 500 Index mutual fund actually earns the same return. We thought that all index funds would match the index. But they are just close, not perfect. Of course we recommend that you pick the funds with the best returns. How can you select the funds with the highest returns? (It is undesirable to switch funds in the future, because that will mean realizing your capital gains.) The best approach is to select a fund that has been closely matching the market in the past. Several magazines print tables of mutual fund results. On the Internet the one-year, three-year, five-year and ten-year total returns are available for all funds at www.Fidelity.com. And we will post news about index funds and their total returns on www.total-wealth.com. In addition, there is a list of useful web sites in Appendix C.

Also, note the Front-end Loads and Redemption Fees. A mutual fund's total return includes the fund's expense ratio. But front-end loads and redemption fees will reduce the total return. (However, do not over worry about small differences in fees or returns. With $10,000 invested, a return difference of 0.10% is worth $10 per year.)

S&P 500 Index Funds, in order by 3-year return[1]

Symbol	Name	Inception Date	Total Assets (Mil.)	3-Year Return
VFINX	VANGUARD 500 INDEX FUND	8/31/76	110,526	17.58%
USSPX	USAA S&P 500 INDEX FUND	5/1/96	3,026	17.38%
FSMKX	FIDELITY SPART MARKET INDEX	3/6/90	10,715	17.34%
HLEIX	ONE GROUP-EQUITY INDEX FD-I	7/2/91	1,855	17.27%
PREIX	T ROWE PRICE EQUITY INDEX 500	3/30/90	5,049	17.25%
VTGIX	VANGUARD TAX-MANAGED G&I	9/6/94	2,240	17.17%
SPY	SPYDERS, S&P 500 DEPOSITORY RECEIPTS	1/29/93	22,845	17.13%
DSPIX	DREYFUS BASIC S&P 500 STK I	9/30/93	2,370	17.12%
ILCIX	GALAXY II LARGE CO INDEX-RET	10/1/90	830	17.12%
SWPIX	SCHWAB S&P 500 FUND-INV SHRS	5/1/96	3,478	17.10%
MASRX	MERRILL LY S&P 500 INDEX-A	4/3/97	883	17.05%
SINEX	STRONG INDEX 500 FUND	5/1/97	139	17.00%
OGEAX	ONE GROUP-EQUITY INDEX FD-A	2/18/92	941	16.99%
PEOPX	DREYFUS S&P 500 INDEX FUND	1/2/90	3,254	16.91%
KNIDX	KENT INDEX EQUITY FD-INVEST	12/1/92	48	16.91%
MUXAX	MUNDER INDEX 500 FUND-CL A	12/9/92	393	16.85%
NOSIX	NORTHERN STOCK INDEX FUND	10/7/96	528	16.83%
NEIAX	NATIONS LARGE CAP INDEX-INVA	10/10/95	29	16.83%
BTEIX	WACHOVIA EQUITY INDEX FUND-A	5/7/93	182	16.67%
SSTIX	VICTORY STOCK INDEX FUND	12/3/93	878	16.59%
SFCSX	WELLS FARGO EQUITY INDEX-A	1/25/84	623	16.41%
BTIEX	BT INVESTMENT EQTY 500 INDEX	12/31/92	953	16.00%
SCPIX	SCUDDER S&P 500 INDEX FUND-S	8/29/97	321	15.62%
SVSPX	SSGA S&P 500 INDEX FUND	12/30/92	2,443	15.20%
SBSPX	SMITH BARNEY S&P 500 INDEX SHR	1/2/98	358	NA
ISPIX	INVESCO S&P 500 INDEX-II	12/23/97	90	NA

S&P 500 Index Funds, in order by 3-year return[1]

Symbol	Front End Load (%)	Expense Ratio (%)	Redemption Fee (%)	Min Invest	Min IRA Invest	Phone Number
VFINX		0.18		3,000	1,000	800-662-7447
USSPX		0.18		3,000	2,000	800-382-8722
FSMKX		0.19		10,000	500	800-544-8888
HLEIX		0.35		1,000	250	800-480-4111
PREIX		0.40	0.50	2,500	1,000	800-638-5660
VTGIX		0.19	2.00	10,000	NA	800-662-7447
SPY		0.12		13,000	13,000	800-843-2639
DSPIX		0.20		10,000	1,000	800-645-6561
ILCIX		0.47		2,500	100	800-628-0414
SWPIX		0.35		2,500	1,000	800-435-4000
MASRX		0.38		100	500	800-637-3863
SINEX		0.45		2,500	1,000	800-368-1030
OGEAX	5.25	0.60		1,000	250	800-480-4111
PEOPX		0.50	1.00	2,500	750	800-373-9387
KNIDX		0.66		1,000	1,000	800-633-5368
MUXAX	2.50	0.44		250	250	800-438-5789
NOSIX		0.55		2,500	500	800-595-9111
NEIAX		0.60		1,000	500	800-321-7854
BTEIX	5.75	0.69		250	250	800-994-4414
SSTIX	5.75	0.81		500	100	800-539-3863
SFCSX	5.75	0.71		1,000	250	800-222-8222
BTIEX		0.25		2,500	500	800-730-1313
SCPIX		0.40		2,500	1,000	800-225-2470
VSPX		0.18		1,000	250	800-647-7327
SBSPX		0.59		1,000	250	800-451-2010
ISPIX		0.60		5,000	2,000	800-525-8085

Appendix A

Suggested Reading List

HERE ARE A FEW GOOD BOOKS. The subject of each book is explained in the comment.

- Robert T. Kiyosaki, *Rich Dad, Poor Dad*. Techpress, 1997. 195 pages. This book explains how to own assets that increase your total wealth and avoid owning liabilities. An excellent companion to *Total Wealth*.

- Thomas J. Stanley, William D. Danko, *The Millionaire Next Door*. Pocket Books, 1996. 255 pages. This book tells how ordinary people saved vast amounts of money. It is excellent if you wish to find ways to increase your savings rate.

- Suze Orman, *The 9 Steps to Financial Freedom*. Crown, 1997. 285 pages. This book will improve your attitude about wealth. Learn how to live with and attract wealth, starting where you are today.

- George S. Clason, *The Richest Man in Babylon*. Signet, 1926. 144 pages. This fable has inspired many to start planning their financial future.

Appendix A

- Jeremy J. Siegel, *Stocks for the Long Run*. McGraw-Hill, 1998. 290 pages. This examination of 200 years of stock prices clearly shows that stocks outperform all other financial assets over the long run.

- Burton G. Malkiel, *A Random Walk Down Wall Street*, Revised 1999. W.W. Norton, 1973. 460 pages. This book started the Random Walk Theory of investing. The Random Walk Theory is that passive management, investing in the market index, will outperform most market participants.

- William J. O'Neil, *How to Make Money in Stocks*. McGraw-Hill, 1995. 257 pages. This book presents O'Neil's system for picking winning stocks. If you want to invest in stocks, this book contains many valuable insights. O'Neil is a momentum investor. Momentum investors are active managers who buy stocks that are rising in price, expecting that the rising trend will continue.

- Benjamin Graham, *The Intelligent Investor*. Harper Business, 1973. 328 pages. This is the classic bestseller on value investing. Value investors are active managers who buy undervalued stocks, expecting that their prices will rise in the future.

APPENDIX B

Leasing or Buying a Car

IN CHAPTER 6, "THE ENDOWMENT LIFESTYLE," we discussed paying cash for a car or borrowing to buy a car. The third option is leasing a car.

If we compare a car loan to a lease, the loan is for the entire price of the car—for example, $20,000 for three years at 8%. The final value of the car after three years is the residual value, say 60% of the purchase price, $12,000. When the car loan is paid, the borrower owns the car.

A lease is like two loans. On the $8,000 depreciation, the lessor pays interest and repays the $8,000 principal. On the $12,000 residual value, the lessor pays interest only. At the end of the lease, returning the car returns the $12,000 residual value to the leasing company. In contrast, on a $20,000 car loan the borrower pays interest and repays the $20,000 principal. Therefore, lease payments are typically much lower than loan payments. Also, in a lease the sales tax is paid only on the portion of each monthly payment that depreciates. With a loan (since you are buying the car) sales tax is paid on the full price at the start.

In the Car Lease example below, the "Depreciation Fee" of $222.22 is the monthly repayment of the three-year, $8,000 loan at

8%. The "Lease Fee" of $106.67 is the monthly interest only payment on the three-year, $12,000 loan at 8%. The sum of these two, plus the Usage Tax, is the monthly lease payment $348.62.

In the Car Loan example below, the monthly loan payment is $644.33. That is $295.71 more than the monthly lease payment.

Car Lease Numbers	36 months, 8% interest
Lease Price:	$20,000.00 (above minus $ 0 down payment)
Residual Value:	$12,000.00 (after 36 months)
Up Front Fees:	$610.00 ($125.00 MV, $135.00 Documents, $350.00 Acquisition Fee)
Depreciation Fee:	$222.22 - Depreciation portion of lease payment
Lease Fee:	$106.67 - Residual Value portion of lease payment
Monthly Payment :	$328.89 without tax
Usage Tax:	$19.73 over full loan (6.00% of $8,000.00)
Total Monthly Payment:	$348.62 WHAT YOU PAY
Total 3-year payments	$13,160.32

Car Loan Numbers	36 months, 8% interest
Cost:	$20,000.00
Cost plus tax:	$21,200.00 ($1,200.00 at 6%)
Up-front Fees:	$260.00 ($125.00 Motor Vehicles Fee, $135.00)
Total Monthly Payment:	$664.33 WHAT YOU PAY
Total 3-year payments	$24,175.88
Minus Value of Car	-$12,000.00
Total Cost of Loan	$12,175.88

The loan costs more on a monthly basis, but in the end you own a $12,000 car. In total, the lease costs $985 more than the loan ($13,160–$12,175 = $985). However, if you put the $295.71 monthly savings from the lease into your PEA earning 12% to 15%, it would earn about $12,800 during the three-year period. So the lease appears advantageous if we have the difference invested in our PEA. But let's look at the lifestyle differences between a lease and a loan.

Lease Problems

With a car lease, the leasing company is the owner of the car, and you lease it from them. On the last day of the lease you no longer have a car. That means that you must buy another car before the lease runs out. In addition, the car lease can't be paid off early. If you move to a city, or get married, or no longer want the car, you can't sell it because you don't own it. The only way to get out of a lease early is to find someone with good credit to take over the lease payments. Also, the lease specifies mileage limits, such as 12,000 miles per year. If you drive more than the specified mileage, then you owe mileage charges. Finally, when you return the car at the end of the lease, any excessive wear, dents, or scratches must be paid for. Also, there is a lease acquisition fee at the start of each lease (typically $350).

Loan Advantages

In contrast to the car lease, with a car loan you own the car. The lender makes the loan to you, with the car as collateral for the loan. When the loan is paid, you own the car and can continue to drive until an attractive opportunity to purchase the next vehicle presents itself. Also, if you wish to sell the car before the loan is paid off, you simply sell the car and repay the bank the remainder of the loan. There are no mileage charges or wear and tear deductions. With a car you do have to pay the full sales tax at the start, but you do not have to pay a lease acquisition fee.

The cost of having to buy a car on a certain day can be very high. If your lease terminates in November, when the showrooms are filled with new cars, you may find a nice car, but pay a high price for it. If you had a car loan, you could continue to drive until you find the car you want at the price you want. At the end of January, many car dealers offer cash rebates and low financing rates to sell cars. Promotions featuring 0% financing, 3.5% financing, or 6% financing are common when cars go on sale. Sometimes you can negotiate a low price for the car and a low interest rate on the financing. A car lease gives you no option to terminate early or late. As we said before, choices are worth money. Keeping your option to choose when you want to switch cars can be worth money. If you save 5% on financing a $20,000 car, that is $3,000 over three years.

So what we want is the flexibility of owning our car, and low monthly payments.

Comparing the Lease and the Loan

As we saw above, the lease costs more overall, but less each month. We want those low monthly payments, but we want the flexibility to sell our car whenever we want. How can we get the low monthly payments of the lease, with the advantages of the loan? We can come close by comparing a three-year lease to a five-year loan. The five-year loan has lower payments, and if we pay off the five-year loan by selling the car after three years, it looks and smells like a three-year lease without the disadvantages. This brings the monthly loan payment down from $664.33 to $429.99. The loan payments are still larger than the lease, but you may think that the added flexibility of owning your own car is worth the difference. The total cost of this loan after three years is $13,239.39.

New Car Loan Numbers	60 months, 8% interest
Cost:	$20,000.00
Cost plus tax	$21,200.00 ($1,200.00 at 6%)
Up Front Fees	$260.00 ($125.00 Motor Vehicles Fee, $135.00 Documents)
Total Monthly Payment	**$429.86** WHAT YOU PAY
Total 3-year payments	**$15,474.96**
Total cost of the loan	**$13,239.36** ($15,474.96 - $12,000.00 + $9,504.40 (Loan Cost *minus* final value of the car *plus* balance due on the loan after three years)

	3-year Lease	3-year Loan	5-year Loan Paid Off in 3 Years	Do Not Buy a Car
Cost of Car	$20,000.00	$20,000.00	$20,000.00	$0.00
Up-front Costs	$610.00	$260.00	$260.00	$0.00
Monthly Payment	$348.62	$664.33	$429.86	$0.00
Cost after 36 payments	$13,160.32	$24,175.88	$15,734.96	$0.00
Final Value of Car	$0.00	$12,000.00	$12,000.00	$0.00
Balance Due on Loan	$0.00	$0.00	$9,504.40	$0.00
Payments - Value of Car + Balance	**$13,160.32**	**$12,175.88**	**$13,239.36**	**$0.00**
Starting PEA	$20,000.00	$20,000.00	$20,000.00	$20,000.00
Invest Up-front Cost Savings	$0.00	$450.00	$450.00	$610.00
Invest Monthly Payment Savings of	$315.71	$0.00	$234.47	$664.33
Total Invested (36 payments)	$11,365.56	$0.00	$8,440.92	$23,915.88
Growth in PEA at 14.88%	$12,966.30	$10,550.58	$12,517.10	$16,204.91
Final Value of PEA after 36 Months	**$44,331.86**	**$31,000.58**	**$41,408.02**	**$60,730.79**
Final PEA Minus Cost of the Car	$31,171.54	$18,824.70	$28,168.66	$60,730.79
Monthly Payment/ Investment	$664.33	$664.33	$664.33	$664.33

Looking at this spreadsheet that compares the benefits of the three-year lease, the three-year loan, the five-year loan paid off after three years, and not buying a car at all, we see that the lease gives us the highest PEA value after three years, $44,331.81. The five-year loan paid off after three years comes in about $3,000 behind the lease.

Finding the Loan or the Lease

Almost all banks offer car loans. Now you can obtain a car loan on the Internet without ever visiting anyone in person. However, these loans are usually at the market rate. Automobile manufacturers frequently promote special loan and lease rates to sell cars, such as 5%, 3%, or 0%. However, the car manufacturers only offer these special rates for limited periods of time. In addition, the advertised rates are often not available on the car that you want to buy. Car loans on the Internet can be found at www.peoplefirst.com or by entering "car loan" into any Internet search engine.

Calculating the Lease Payment

Unfortunately, many car salesmen have been taking advantage of people who do not have a lease calculator. You can find a lease calculator on the Internet at www.interest.com/hugh/calc/lease.cgi and www.leaseguide.com/calc.htm. In addition, the car salesperson will print the lease calculation for you, if you insist. There are six variables in a lease calculation: car price, interest rate (or money factor **X** 24), residual value, down payment, up-front fees, and monthly payment. In the example above, a salesman could tell you that your down payment is $2,000, and your monthly payment is $348. Only if you had a lease calculator would you realize that he had just raised the price by $2,000. Therefore, never agree to a lease until you have run the calculations yourself. It may help if you run your estimate of the lease calculations before the final negotiation, and bring the printouts with you. Then you will spot any major deviations immediately.

APPENDIX C
Web Sites (www.total-wealth.com)

THIS STORY IS NOT OVER. Many of you will ask questions. New securities will be issued that index investors will want to use. This book will be continued on the Internet at www.total-wealth.com. There we can present new topics, respond to questions, and provide current information about developments that will be relevant to readers of the book.

A book is much nicer to read than a web site. People can carry it, read it, write on it, and refer back to it in the future. But the drawback of the printed page is that it cannot change. The Internet will allow us to provide updates.

In addition, there are several other good web sites where you can learn more about investing. Here is a list that we recommend as a start.

www.bloomberg.com	Financial News, Investment Tracking
www.vanguard.com	Financial Planning Information
www.fidelity.com	Mutual Fund Information
www.quicken.com	Investment Tracking, Planning
www.morningstar.com	Investment Information
www.fairmark.com	Roth IRA information
www.about.com	Articles on Financial Topics

NOTES

Chapter 1

[1] Burton G. Malkiel, *A Random Walk Down Wall Street*, New York: W.W. Norton, 1973 and 1999.
[2] Benjamin Graham, *The Intelligent Investor*, Harper Business, 1973.

Chapter 2

[1] Jonathan Burton, *Bloomberg Personal Finance*, July/August 1998, p. 70.
[2] As of 12/31/99, source www.fidelity.com.
[3] As of 6/30/00, source www.fidelity.com.
[4] Source: Vanguard Group.

Chapter 3

[1] Burton G. Malkiel, *A Random Walk Down Wall Street*, New York: W.W. Norton, 1999, p. 262.

Chapter 4

[1] Jeremy J. Siegel, *Stocks for the Long Run,* New York: MacMillan, 1998, p. 6.

[2] Jeremy J. Siegel, *Stocks for the Long Run,* New York: MacMillan, 1998, p. 13 and p. 15.

[3] Jeremy J. Siegel, *Stocks for the Long Run,* New York: MacMillan, 1998, p. 13 and p. 15.

Chapter 8

[1] Standard & Poor's, S&P 500 Directory 1997. Standard & Poor's, p. 6.

Chapter 11

[1] Warren Buffett, Berkshire Hathaway, "Letter to Shareholders 1997," http://www.berkshirehathaway.com/letters/1997.html

[2] "In the Vanguard" newsletter 1998, No. 3, p. 3, Vanguard Marketing Corporation.

Chapter 17

[1] "In the Vanguard" newsletter, 1998, No. 3, p. 3., Vanguard Marketing Corporation.

Chapter 32

[1] Three-year return from 10/31/97 to 10/31/00, data from Bloomberg Financial Markets.

Acknowledgments

MANY THANKS ARE DUE to Mike Bloomberg, senior partner at Bloomberg Financial Markets. I have worked for Mike for twenty-two years and he has always encouraged me in everything that I wished to do. After he wrote a book, *Bloomberg by Bloomberg*, he introduced his book agent to me and encouraged my efforts in this book.

Thanks are also due to Bloomberg Financial Markets. The company has helped with publicity on this book, and provided the laptop computer that allowed me to write it on the bus. In addition, all the raw data came from The Bloomberg Terminal.

I must thank Olympia Trails Bus Company for providing a ninety-minute ride to and from Manhattan every day, and filling the surrounding seats with stockbrokers, mutual fund managers, traders, and investment bankers. In this milieu, any question on the markets could be answered firsthand, with humor thrown in at no extra charge.

INDEX

active fund managers, 147–49;
beating the market and, 118,
173–74; experience and, 163;
as momentum investors, 220;
passive index fund investors vs.,
109; stocks vs. index funds and,
159–60; as value investors, 220
alternative investments, 105–8
American Stock Exchange, 214
*A Random Walk Down Wall
Street* (Malkiel), 5, 220
asset allocation: compound returns
and, 4–5, 14; credit card debt
and, 165–66; long-term investments and, 43–44
assets, 52–55
automatic investment plans, 120,
122, 208
average equity managers, index
funds vs., 29(t)

BAA bond rating, 106–7
baby boomers, retirement of,
176–77

bank certificates of deposit, 39–40
Barnes, Mac, vii
bear markets, 92, 95
Bible, 127, 180
Bloomberg, Michael, vii
Bloomberg Forum, 6
board of trustees, 171
Boeing, 212
bonds: consistency of, 32; long-
term investments vs., 108,
170–71; returns on, 32(t), 33(t),
34(t), 105(t); rolling principle
into, 134–35; stocks vs., 31–34,
105–6, 133, 175; taxable
income from, 171; volatility of,
133; yields from, 160
borrowing: collateral and, 45–46;
for college education, 63, 209;
endowment lifestyle and,
48–51, 55–56, 58–60; limits to,
45, 55–56, 58; manageable
debts and, 45; PEAs and,
58–60, 209–10; taxes and, 193.
See also margin borrowing

235

INDEX

Vanguard Index Trust 500
(VFINX) (*continued*) largest
mutual fund, 173; S&P 500
Stock Index and, 5–6; taxable
capital gains distributions by,
6; total return and performance of, 6(t); turnover of, 6, 16

Washington, George, 48–49
wealth: accumulation of, 3, 37,
166, 179; choices and, 164;
leaving to heirs of, 143–45;
total, 12
web sites, 229
Wellington Mutual Fund, 86
Western Union Telegraph, 159
women, as money managers,
163–64

Woolworth, 159
www.about.com, 229
www.bloomberg.com, 229
www.fairmark.com, 229
www.fidelity.com, 215, 229
*www.interest.com/hugh/calc/lease.
cgi*, 227
www.leaseguide.com/calc.htm,
227
www.morningstar.com, 229
www.peoplefirst.com, 227
www.quicken.com, 229
www.total-wealth.com, 211, 215,
229
www.vanguard.com, 229